THE KEY TO SURVIVAL
Interpersonal Communication

Tom Fisher
Tracey L. Smith
Lewis and Clark Community College

WAVELAND
PRESS, INC.
Prospect Heights, Illinois

For information about this book, write or call:
    Waveland Press, Inc.
    P.O. Box 400
    Prospect Heights, Illinois 60070
    (312) 634-0081

Copyright © 1987 by Waveland Press, Inc.

ISBN 0-88133-257-7

Printed in the United States of America

Dedicated to
Pat Goehe

TABLE OF CONTENTS

PREFACE

Hello. Let us introduce ourselves to you. We are Tom Fisher and Tracey Smith, the authors of this textbook. We wanted to take this opportunity to try and communicate with you on a more personal level than is available in most traditional "texts."

We are two human beings with families, friends, jobs, social lives, problems and joys—just as you are. In fact, it is our very "humanness" that led us to write this text. We believe from our experiences in life (combined, that't over 80 years at this business called "life"!) that we have not only learned that it has been effective communication that has enriched those experiences, but also has provided us with the tools necessary to survive in this world.

In all instances, whether it has been a success in the personal or professional arenas, it has been the use of this key that has rewarded our endeavors. We are also painfully aware of the times when our ineffectual communication has led us into conflict, difficulties, and emotional trauma. Because of this and because we are teachers by vocation and avocation, we hoped that in writing this book we could share some of what we've learned through study and experience. You will find this book full of our personal anecdotes and stories used to give you examples. We have done this for a reason. We believe that while we are all unique, we all share commonalities and by sharing our experiences with you, you will be more easily able to identify with what we are talking about. Throughout these pages that follow we have tried to talk with you as we would if you were in our classroom or visiting with us in our offices or homes. We do not offer the definitive study of interpersonal communication, nor do we claim to have all the answers. What we do hope you find is a better understanding of this very important process that we tend to take for granted called "communication." There is a lot to be learned, but it's up to you to take the initiative. We hope this text helps you in your attempt to survive in this complicated environment we call our world.

Nothing of this kind can be undertaken without the help of some very special people. We would like to take this opportunity to thank some of those whose help and encouragement have made this book possible. First, our students, families and friends provided the material for us to examine and learn from. Next, we recognize our colleagues at Lewis and Clark College who have answered our questions and provided that "pat on the back" or the "kick in the pants" as the occasion warranted. To Mary Vaughne goes our gratitude for shepherding this project through the word-processor. And finally, to our good friend, Neil Rowe, a toast for without his encouragement the project would not have been attempted in the first place.

We hope you enjoy the fruits of our labors and gain some insight into how you communicate (or fail to communicate) as you do.

1

Introductions, Assumptions, and Definitions

I. The Introduction.
   A. Communication has a long history.
   B. Communication is an ongoing behavior.
   C. Examples will come from many areas of life.

II. Assumptions.
   A. This class is not a "bag of tricks."
   B. We shall speak of "efficient" and "inefficient" communication.
   C. Communication takes time.
   D. Communication is an everchanging process.
   E. The relationship must continue.
   F. You wish to express yourself with a minimum of harm to others.
   G. Some communication problems cannot be resolved.

III. Definitions.
   A. A model includes "sender" and "receiver."
   B. The model is enlarged to include "feedback."
   C. The model is extended to include "environment" and "noise."

IV. Communication is motivated by our basic needs.
   A. We all have physical needs.
   B. We all require a degree of security.
   C. We have social needs.
   D. We have self-esteem needs.
   E. We all wish to achieve "self-actualization."

V. Four elements are needed for "efficient" messages.
   A. Share the specific incident you are reacting to.
   B. Share your reaction to the incident.
   C. Share your feelings about the incident.
   D. Seek feedback from your partner.

Introduction

The history of mankind is the history of communication. From the earliest records we find men trying to express their basic needs, fears, joys, and frustrations about their conditions. We find that the major difference between mankind and other mammals in the animal kingdom is the ability to talk. Often this talk has gotten us (and our tribes) into trouble: disputes over boundaries, lawsuits regarding property, squabbles about inheritance—all as a result of our ability (of lack of it) to communicate our thoughts, feelings and ideas.

From the time a child first learns to produce sound, she is expressing herself and her impressions of the world around her. If you have forgotten just how much children talk, pass a playground at recess and just listen to the sounds emanating from the many throats indicating the efforts of the young people to coerce, to argue, to placate, to demand. Yes, we as parents are sometimes shocked when our child repeats a ploy or a gambit that she has heard at home. She uses the same devices of communication she has seen in operation in the family circle. As a child overhears her parents arguing about the payment of a bill at the breakfast table, she translates those words and situations into her own experience and we adults hear our own words coming out of her mouth in her attempt to express her delight, frustration, or power in relations with her playmates. Communication is an ongoing behavior. It starts in infancy and continues throughout our lives. It is essential in some form to basic survival.

You have enrolled in a course in "interpersonal communication." Exactly what does this mean? You may be thinking "I have been alive for years. I am a member of a society which demands my verbal and non-verbal responses on subjects ranging from what television show I wish to watch all the way to what I would like to eat for dinner. I have been engaging in *interpersonal communication* all my life." Very true. So, why take a course concerning such a skill? The reason may become clear if we offer a hypothetical situation which may sound familiar.

You have been invited to a party. The guests will be people you don't know. The hostess assures you that you will meet some "very interesting" people and urges you to attend. How will you react when you get to that party? Are you the type of person who stands in a corner by the punch bowl and the hors d'oeuvres tray waiting for one of those "interesting" people to come over and strike up a conversation? Or are you the type who can walk up to someone who is unknown to you and begin to talk? What are the first things you will say to that person? What topics can you choose which will give a good impression of you and put your partner at ease? How familiar can you get and how fast? Suppose you are rebuffed. Do you immediately head for the coat rack, bid your hostess good-bye and head out into the night?

We have all been in similar situations. Sometimes we handle ourselves quite well. We are in a good mood. The conversation may start slowly, but soon we are chatting away with our new friend as if we had known her all our life. When we approach a stranger who is depressed, can we say something which will bring him out of himself and allow him to enjoy the party with us? What marks a good "party goer"? Why are some people just "naturals" at making friends? Are they just smarter than we are? Are they show-offs or stage-hoggers who are only concerned with an audience for their new stories? Why can't some people realize how nervous we are and treat us with more sensitivity? Why are some people so hard to get to know? These and many other questions which come to us at the start of the party are the raw materials of this course. And we shall be looking at a lot more situations than attending parties. Perhaps you have occasionally asked yourself "How can I express myself more clearly, less defensively, more honestly? How can I be more receptive to the needs and attitudes of others?" All of the above questions deal with the principles of interpersonal communication and will be addressed in this text. We shall deal with situations at work, at home, at school, at play—all of which involve your relations with other people. We shall relate some of the experiences of scholars and teachers, managers and workers, parents and children, husbands and wives to see how they fail or succeed in the business we call "communicating."

Our investigation will take us into many areas of our experience and we urge the students and their faculty to be forthcoming and open in sharing what problems they have had in these areas and how they solved or attempted to solve them. Many of you will shun this "open discussion" technique. You believe yourself shy and not worthy of discussion. What could possibly be gained by telling the class that you just had a fight with your boyfriend or your child? One observation we have made over the years of teaching this class is that although the names and circumstances may change, the problems of communication remain constant, and by discussing these problems (which are common to all who breathe) we can find satisfactory solutions to many of them. We can see in the light of investigation and sharing what went sour, and often we can offer suggestions to correct or at least improve the circumstances. Before we continue, let's set forth some guidelines we call "assumptions" to help give us some format from which we can view this often confusing discipline of speech communication.

Assumptions

1. This class is not a "bag of tricks" to give you the upper hand in dealing with your family and friends. Many people who take this course get the idea that communication skills are somehow "magic" which provide the one who knows the "tricks" some kind of advantage in any conversation. If I know the rules better than my opponent, then I should *win*! There are two things wrong with such an attitude. First of all, communication is regarded in this text as a mutual activity, between and among people—not one person *against* another or group. A person should gain as much from an exchange of thoughts, feelings, and ideas as he contributes. As human beings we are involved in relationships; we are not billiard balls bumping against one another on an endless pool table. Secondly, our goal is to reach a consensus of ideas and solutions, not just acquiescence. If I am having a political discussion with a friend, I am seeking information about how he views the situation as well as sharing my views. I can learn and grow with such an exchange. If I just spout my own carefully held, thoroughly understood beliefs without regard for my fellow participant in the discussion, I become a fanatical bigot and a social liability. Without tolerance for others' views, I become an actor giving a monologue, not a true communicator. This is not to imply that we are not entitled to our own opinions. We are. But so are others. By sharing ideas (a give-and-take) we can learn and understand ourselves and others better.

2. The operative words we shall use for an exchange are "efficient" or "inefficient," not "good" or "bad." As we investigate the various problems we and our friends have in communicating, we shall assess the degree of satisfaction gained by the parties involved: Did they clearly send the message? Was my message received in the spirit in which it was sent? Did both parties come away from the exchange with a feeling of self-worth? Obviously, such questions imply "good" or "bad," but we have found that eliminating the value judgment words gives our investigation more objectivity and clarity. How would you evaluate the following exchange?

The story is told of a man who was raising beans in a field next to a farmer's pasture where a horse was grazing. One night the horse jumped the fence and galloped through the bean patch. The horse owner went to get his erring animal from the bean patch and just as he was leading the horse back across the fence, the bean farmer appeared and asked, "What are you going to do about the damage to my beans?" The horse owner, already embarrassed by the damage the horse had done, replied simply and defensively, "Sue me!" The exchange was *inefficient*. The simple request of the bean farmer for retribution was misunderstood by the horse owner who cut off future communication with the threat of a law suit. Later we'll discuss what other things could have been said by either party, but for our purposes here it is enough to say that this exchange was anything but efficient.

3. Communication takes time. In a world which is so time-conscious with fast-food restaurants, microwave ovens, and computers which have reduced the usual time-consuming activities of food preparation and gathering information from several sources, we are perhaps inclined to become impatient with our families and friends who require time from us simply to be understood. The average television sit-com only needs thirty minutes to resolve its conflict. Yet "real life" is different from "reel life." Look for a moment at the simple matter of instructing a child of two not to cross the street. The adult has a very important message for that child, but the child may not fully understand the message if the adult does not take the time to explain "why" it is important for the child to remain on the same side of the street. Now, we are not suggesting that a full 15-minute discourse on the hazards of street-crossing is necessary for the child, but she would probably like to know "why?" We have observed that children are amazingly understanding (usually) if they are given some facts to back up the order coming from the adult. We have also observed the reticence on the part of parents and other adults who deal frequently with children to give such an explanation. Without the explanation the order makes no sense to the child with her limited experience patterns. She may not understand the danger of being hit by a car. She doesn't drive. She can't read the signs regarding speed limits in sub-divisions. The assumption of the adult is that "any fool ought to know why." Just a simple expenditure of time would clear up this problem of communication. Adults as well as children often need time to understand ideas. All too often we assume that since it is simple and logical to us, others will comprehend it equally well. This is not always true. Therefore, as the exchanges become more involved, more emotionally laden, more time is required to clarify the messages being exchanged.

We also might say here that you will be faced with learning a new skill. While it is true that you have been talking all your life, you may wish to alter some of the ways you communicate and this, also, takes time. We ask our students to try a new technique, and they will return and state that it didn't work. "How long did you try it?" we ask. "All weekend," they'll say. "How long have you been doing it the other way?" "Five, eighteen, thirty years." We might equate the act of trying to change your communication habits with learning a musical instrument or a new sport. The first time out on ice skates you were probably a little wobbly, but you kept at it, and finally you were able to circle the rink without falling. The same is true of these skills. With increased confidence and practice you can master them, too.

4. Communication is a dynamic, everchanging process. In investigating the process itself and the techniques of speech used by ourselves and others, we are really attempting the impossible. We can never recreate exactly the circumstances surrounding any verbal exchange. Even as we begin to focus attention on the "why" rather than the "what" of communication, we alter that communication. We become self-conscious; the emotional values evaporate; the core essence of the original exchange is altered. But, although the situation may alter somewhat under scrutiny, that very altering allows a somewhat more objective analysis of the process under observation. Yes, communication is always changing because those who are participating are constantly shifting positions and changing. In fact, considering the potential for disaster, we think it is astonishing we communicate as well as we do.

5. Most relationships must continue. To accomplish this, communication is essential. Most of our discussions will center around situations and events involving partners who wish problems to be resolved. You are having an argument with your boss. You can walk out, true, and find another job, but usually this alternative is not practical. You want to satisfactorily deal with the problem at hand. Or, perhaps you have had a fight with your mother. Yes, you could move out, but financially that is not an alternative which is feasible at the moment. You must stay and work out a solution to the communication breakdown. In a society which recognizes (even encourages) divorce, many people tend to break relationships rather than seek solutions. Our emphasis in this book remains on finding what went wrong with the communication in the first place, studying both parties who contributed to the breakdown, and checking the external elements which may have caused the misunderstanding at the outset. Most of the time two people can work out their differences if they are given the desire, time and skills to do so. Our work is to find the ways that help clear the air of defensiveness and character assassination and deal with the issues which caused the misunderstanding. Why did my wife blow up when I asked her how much she paid for that new dress? Why did my professor react so violently when I asked her to explain why I didn't get credit for a given answer on a test?

These are questions which can be answered in the light of reason and understanding on the part of both parties involved.

6. You wish to express yourself by causing a minimum of harm to others. They may be as sensitive as you are. In the rush to make yourself understood you may say things which hurt. All communication is not appropriate. There will be times when your partner cannot hear or doesn't want to listen to your message. You need to read the signs. You know when your parents are upset without a word being said. The tension is in the air; the slammed door is hard to ignore. It stands to reason, therefore, that now is not the time to ask to borrow the family car for Friday night's date. When your husband hits the front door at 5:30 p.m. in a foul mood, you know enough not to mention that your little son stopped up the toilet by flushing a diaper down it. These cautions seem obvious, but we have found that the relationships which last and bring satisfaction to both parties are those which include sensitivity to the partner without sacrificing respect for self. We are all basically selfish. Decisions we make are usually made egotistically. As babies we were indulged and pampered, but sociologists tell us that the socialization process we go through as we mature includes becoming aware of others and their needs. We all know people who respond as if they never went through that process. They react as if their needs are the only needs to be considered. But we also know the others, those who are "other-oriented." The ideal to keep in mind is a delicate balance between freedom of expression and an understanding of and respect for the sensibilities of the fellow-communicator.

7. There are certain times when a communication problem can't be resolved. When your partner becomes adamant, or you become stubborn, there may not be a solution to the breakdown. It would be unrealistic of us to suggest that all communication can be beneficial. Sometimes compromise is impossible; the price in terms of self-esteem or principles is too high. We need to recognize when these situations occur and simply move on. The dire effects of an unresolved conflict may be recriminations and name-calling, but they, too, can be avoided. You and your partner, for the moment at least, agree to disagree.

These six assumptions, then, will stand as check-points for our future discussions about the principles of interpersonal communication. Keep them in mind as we try to define and explain the complex process of exchanges between people.

Definitions

To clarify the process of interpersonal communication perhaps a model will help: "A" wishes to send a message to "B":

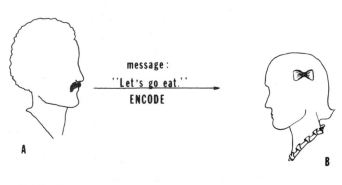

© Alice M. Lake

The sender, "A," must first *encode* that message. Encoding is the process of turning a mental image into a symbol that you believe the other person will be able to understand. He must then choose a *channel* (the air, a telephone, etc.) through which to send his message. When the receiver, "B," gets the message, she must then decode it (decoding is the process of turning a symbol back into a mental image), decide upon a response, and send "A" *feedback* (message varification).

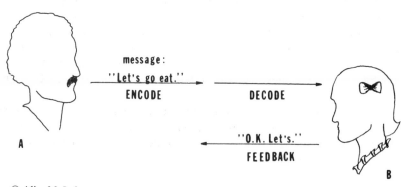

© Alice M. Lake

All very simple. Why, then, are so many messages misunderstood? Perhaps we can add some elements to the model which may explain the difficulty.

© Alice M. Lake

You will note that the third model includes two elements not present in the other two models: *environment* and *noise*. "Environment" refers to the individual's point of view made up of her background, language, culture, experience—all the things that make that individual unique. If I, as an Episcopalian, am engaged in a discussion of religious issues with a Roman Catholic, our environments overlap. Both of us are "catholics"; both of us observe a "Mass"; both of us share the doctrine of "apostolic succession." But we differ in our points of view about all three of those items. Therefore, if we are to continue our discussion, we must recognize these differences. Or, take the situation of a child talking to a parent. Both are (or have been) children, but the relative point of view of both is different. For the two of them to clearly understand one another each must appreciate the other's point of view (environment).

Another element which may figure in the communication is *noise*. Noise is any interference with listening or hearing what is said. Three types of noise may be present: physical noise, external noise, and internal noise. Physical noise refers to a hearing problem, some loss (permanent or temporary) of the organ of reception, use of a hearing aid, etc. External noise refers to extraneous sound which may be present at the exchange of the message like a loud band, a TV set, other people talking, or even an overheated room. These can interfere with the sending or receiving of a message. Internal noise is more complex to describe. It refers to a preoccupation on the part of the receiver. How often have you tried to send a message to someone who is not paying attention to you? Your partner

may have been thinking of something else and did not consciously hear you, or the subject of the message was such that he could not accept it. An alcoholic, for example, may not be able to discuss the subject of temperance. Or, someone who has just lost a loved one in an automobile crash may not be able to discuss the subject of death. Noise, then, can play a large part in the communication process.

Important as all these foregoing elements are, there is another element which plays a great part in communication. That element is "self-image," what a person thinks of himself. Each message we send includes the information about how we feel about ourselves at the moment we send the message. We shall take up the various ways of reading these "self-image messages" in the next chapter, but we would like you to keep in mind that this element definitely exists in the exchange.

Motivation for Communication: Maslow's Hierarchy of Needs

Having put forth a symbol of the communication process with the models, let us now look to the reasons and ways we use communication for our survival. To understand why we behave as we do in terms of our communication perhaps we should examine the needs that we, as human beings, share with one another.

Abraham Maslow, noted psychologist, has arranged the needs we have in five major categories. The categories range from our most basic physical concerns as creatures to the most sophisticated psychological and philosophical requirements. Each level of needs requires communication to satisfy the needs listed, and movement from one step on the hierarchy to the next also requires communication skills. One cannot progress from one level to the next until the needs of the initial levels are met. In ascending order the steps on Maslow's need chart are as follows: physical needs, security needs, social needs, self-esteem needs, and finally the area Maslow terms "self-actualization." Let's look at each step individually and suggest ways that our communication helps us to satisfy the various needs to survive in our world.

Physical Needs: This is the basic step we start on as infants and we must continue to satisfy the needs in this area throughout our lives. It includes such considerations as food, air, water and bodily comfort. How does a baby satisfy these needs? She cries, a very effective means of communication particularly at 3 a.m. As she grows, she learns language and is able to tell her adult protectors very specifically what she desires: "I don't like carrots!" "Daddy, please stop the car. I need to tinkle." And we know this about children (though we tend to forget it when we become adults): there is no discussing anything of importance at bedtime. When the child cannot hold his eyes open, do not try to "reason" with him. First things must come first. Satisfy the need for sleep, and then discuss why he should not have hit his sister.

Security Needs: This is the area which deals with shelter and the need to feel safe, the reason we lock our doors at night. Recently, there has been much discussion in the media concerning elderly people who feel prisoners in their urban dwellings because they do not feel safe stepping out to take a stroll. Part of this need is addressed through our relationships with family and close friends, the need to be able to depend upon the strength of a relationship. Communication is needed here in the form of reassurance we receive from others that "things are going go be all right." It can also be as simple as reminding ourselves or someone else that the weather has changed and a jacket is now needed to protect us from the elements.

Social Needs: From the security needs, we progress to the category of personal contacts. People cannot live alone. Most of us need companionship and evidence of affection. We seek approval early as children and continue to feel the need of family and peer acceptance throughout our personal and working lives. Skill in communication here is essential because we must now begin to share and concern ourselves with others' needs as well. To have a friend we must be a friend, and this takes communication. When a friend comes with a problem, I must sometimes forsake my own goals for a moment to listen and share with my partner. Sympathy, understanding, caring, and love are all made possible through honest, sincere communication.

Self-Esteem Needs: As the social needs are being considered and satisfied, we are fulfilling this next and vital area of survival—the need to achieve the feeling of self-worth. The relationships we develop with the help of speech and non-verbal means tend to clarify, reveal and define our own self-concept. Through socialization we are discovering ourselves. We find those contacts most satisfying which allow us to feel good about ourselves. We all know those who have been "uppers" in our lives, people along the way who gave us good strokes and made us feel worthwhile and helped lead us to the pinnacle of Maslow's hierarchy—self-actualization.

Self-Actualization: This is the highest plateau of Maslow's need chart, and it has reference to the point in our lives (often never completely realized) where we are functioning at or near our full potential as creative, caring individuals. Self-actualization, then, is the realization of the goal of producing at our maximum potential. With the other four areas of our needs satisfied, we are integrated into whatever society we have chosen for ourselves, whatever relationships we have developed, whatever career we

have planned and now pursue. You are coming to school. One motivation may be to get a higher paying job. Another may be to relieve social pressures from family which tells you that now you must go to school. Another concern of yours may be to make use of your intellectual skills, to fully realize and exhibit your God-given talents and brains. The final reason stated is functioning at your highest possible potential — self-actualization.

Aristotle suggests you cannot know whether or not a man is "good" until he dies. Only then can a full and complete assessment of his life be made. Up to his death he is in the process of "becoming." The same may be said of this last step in Maslow's pyramid: This is the "becoming" step. Here some of our dreams have been realized and others are still to be dreamed. This is all part of survival. How could we possibly hope to achieve this step or meet this need of self-actualization without the tool of communication?

Sending Efficient Messages

Because communication is necessary to move from step to step on Maslow's scale, let us now try to send some "efficient messages," ones which will include enough information for our partners to really get the picture. We shall here suggest four areas to consider.

1. What are you reacting to? First, you must tell your partner what happened; what he did; what actually took place. You saw him yawn when you suggested a visit to your mother's house. She frowned when you suggested a birthday gift for your friend. He brushed by you and entered the elevator first. Something occurred which could be recorded by video tape if it were available.

2. How did you react? Next, you must offer your interpretation of that action, how things looked from your point of view. What does the action mean to you? Why do you think that your partner acted or reacted in that given way? Was he tired, or did the yawn mean more regarding the visit to Mom's? Tell him how it appeared to *you*.

3. What do you feel about the action? Growing out of the interpretation will be some sort of emotion which you experience. How does his action make you feel? Are you hurt, angry, or frustrated? Reveal the actual emotion you feel.

4. Request feedback: From your point of view what will result from his action? What are the possible consequences? If this action were repeated, what might the outcome be? You may

also wish to share what you will do as a result of your partner's behavior. Or, you may wish to initiate feedback or clarification from your partner. Try to keep this portion of the message non-threatening and non-defensive regarding your partner. With these four elements of an efficient message in mind let's look at some situations and try to frame efficient messages for them.

Exercises for Sending Efficient Messages

Directions: For the following situations frame a message which will include the four elements just discussed for efficient messages. Try, if you can, to keep the messages within 50 words.

Situation: Your child (either sex) is 16 and has decided to exhibit some decision-making power by choosing the hours he/she will come home from a date. You have tried to keep a rather tight rein on your children but feel that perhaps it is time that the child makes some decisions. How will you express your ambivalent feelings to the child?

Situation: A worker under you has been caught stealing. He has no family and has become quite close to you during the time he has worked for you. You have a good working relationship and have occasionally enjoyed a social occasion or two. He needs support, but you feel he has betrayed you. How can your emotions be expressed to him?

Situation: Your partner wishes to get (or have you get) an abortion. The child is illegetimate, but you wish to have the child—even to the point of marrying. How can you share your feelings openly?

Situation: You suspect that your partner is an alcoholic. She/he finally confesses that he needs counsel. Money is at a premium, and you suspect that the alcoholism is merely an escape mechanism used by the partner to avoid responsibility. How can you share your feelings of frustration without destroying your partner's good intentions to get help?

Situation: You have a teacher whom you suspect of "having it in for you." You know by the grape-vine that she is a very proud person particularly where teaching and relationships with students are concerned. How can you share your feelings of helplessness so that both your and her egos remain intact?

Conclusion

If in the previous exercise you were able to send an efficient messsage for the five situations, you are beginning to see how complex this business of interpersonal communication is. Keep those seven assumptions in mind as we proceed. And remember, you and you alone are responsible for the way you communicate and survive.

Bibliography

Anderson, Rob. *Students as Real People.* Rochelle Park, New Jersey: Hayden Book Co., Inc., 1979.

Bernie, Eric. *The Structure and Dynamics of Organization and Groups.* New York: Grove Press, Inc., 1963.

Howell, William. *The Empathic Communicator.* Prospect Heights, IL: Waveland Press, Inc., 1982 (reissued 1986).

Maslow, Abraham. *Motivation and Personality.* 2nd Ed. New York: Harper & Row, 1970.

Rubin, Zick, *Liking and Loving.* New York: Holt, Rinehart, and Winston, 1973.

Zunin, Leonard and Natalie Zunin. *Contact: the First Four Minutes.* Los Angeles: Nash Publishing, 1972.

2

Self-Concept and Defensiveness

I. Everyone's self-concept is formed by several influences.
   A. Our parents.
   B. Significant others.
   C. Peers.
   D. Society.

II. Two aspects of the nature of the self-concept.
   A. The self-concept is subjective.
   B. A healthy self-concept must change, but resists change.

III. The self-concept influences our communication.
   A. Self-fulfilling prophecies show *we* determine the outcome of events.
      1. They may be self-imposed.
      2. They may be imposed from without.
   B. We wish to create a positive self-concept.
      1. Make the change a priority in your life.
      2. Develop the skills to make the change possible.
      3. Stick to your decision to make the change.

IV. We protect our self-concept through defensiveness.
   A. Fight.
   B. Flee.

V. We can limit and overcome defensiveness.
   A. Gibb's list of defensive behaviors.
   B. Gibb's list of supportive behaviors.

Introduction

Who am I?

Where am I?

What am I?

Are these questions the lament of some amnesiac time traveler lost in limbo between time and space? No, they are questions we have all asked ourselves at some time. Knowing who we are, what we believe to be true about ourselves, is an important process we all go through. The categorizing and labeling of our traits, abilities and beliefs all combine to form our self-concept.

Self-concept can be defined as the beliefs a person holds to be true about him or herself. This includes our total environment: what we think we are good at, what we believe we lack, our mental, physical and emotional state. Do you think about yourself as outgoing or shy, mathematically inclined or unable to balance a checkbook? Do you consider yourself to be in good physical condition or overweight? All these and more comprise your self-concept and your self-concept affects how you communicate.

Forming and Reinforcing the Self-Concept

Everyone's self-concept is formed and molded by several different influences. No one is affected or reacts in exactly the same way even if they are exposed to the same circumstances. There are, however, four general categories of influences that have an effect (to some degree) on everyone.

Parents: For our purposes we will define "parents" as the person or persons who raised you from infancy to about five years of age. This may be two biological parents, but does not exclusively refer to our natural parents. As far as our self-concepts are concerned, our parents may be adoptive, a single parent, grandparents, aunts or uncles. Whoever we spent the majority of our time with during our very early growth and development can be considered our parents for the purposes of discovering their effect on our self-concept. Just how do they affect how we think about ourselves?

22

Simply stated, they do this by everything they say and do around us. When we are infants, our only method of communication is non-verbal and sounds that are as yet unfocused in words. We cry because we are hungry, tired, or uncomfortable. How our parents react to these displays for attention, even at this early age, begins to tell us how others feel and act toward us. If our needs are met promptly and with affection, we will begin to form a positive self-concept believing that we are important and worthwhile. As we grow and begin to understand and react more to the world around us, we become even more aware of how our parents feel about us. If they treat us in a manner that implies that they accept us and believe us to be good people, then we will believe that about ourselves as well. A student was asked to write a short paper about the effect his parents had on what he believed to be true about himself. After class he came to me and said, "I don't know what to write; my parents hardly ever talked to me. ..I guess that did tell me a lot, didn't it?" Even when the communication is non-verbal, it affects us. Or, take the example of a parent with her three-year-old who is playing on the floor of the livingroom while mom and a friend talk. The friend says, "Johnny sure plays nicely and quietly. You must not have too much problem with him." Mom replies, "Yeah, well he's my dumb one. His brothers are smarter and more out-going, but at least he isn't much of a bother." Johnny has ears and what his mother has just said will affect how he perceives himself.

Our parent's influence doesn't stop when we turn 5, 16, or even 80. We continue to be influenced by what their opinion would be not only for all their life, but for all our life. People whose parents are dead and no longer able to technically help them perceive themselves, still react to how their parents would have responded. Many of us consciously or subconsciously remain tied to Mom's and Dad's beliefs and opinions even when we are mature adults. The degree of our parent's influence on our self-concept will vary from person to person and may shift in importance at different times in our lives, but their effect is certainly apparent on all of us.

Significant Others: In general, significant others are people with whom we spend a great deal of time and have an influence on how and what we think about ourselves. In addition to this, when we are young, they are usually older than we are by at least five years, but as we grow older, they may be anyone of any age that we have major contact with. People who fall into this category may include grandparents, aunts, uncles, teachers, ministers, priests, babysitters, co-workers, etc. Usually, these people are people we respect and want approval from. If they give us their approval and confirm our feelings of self-worth, we will develop a more positive self-image. The opposite is, of course, true as well. Significant others can and often do influence us just as much (sometimes more) than our parents.

A discussion of significant others would be incomplete without mentioning some*thing* else, that over the past 30 years, has become a "significant other" to most people born after 1950. That thing is the television set, or more specifically the programs that we watch and listen to on the TV. Studies show that children entering kindergarten come to school with thousands of hours of television viewing behind them. Such a large percentage of time must have an effect upon the viewer. And watching television doesn't stop when we go to school and learn to read and write. It has become the great American pastime (the recent growth of homes with VCR's has only increased time spent watching the TV). What we watch and listen to affects our perception of ourselves. Let's take the example of an eight-year-old on Saturday morning. She watches her favorite cartoons in which she is exposed to various ideas and thoughts. Much of children's programming now includes morals, value lessons or other comments about the relationship of the program to real life. Other programs imply certain perceptions and even the commercials imply certain criteria for judging our self-perception. Our eight-year-old will interpret these messages and apply them to herself. If she believes that she does what is considered to be "good," she will have a more positive self-image and vice versa. Another effect that may occur, and advertisers are certainly aware of this, is that as the child sees all the toys and breakfast food commercials, she will interpret these as things "good" children either have, or should have, and begin to assess herself by how many of these things she has.

Adults, too, are influenced by what they see and interpret on their sets. Over the past several years we have seen an increase in the use of the television as a media to spread religious beliefs. These TV preachers and religious programming have had an effect on our self-concepts as well. By their very nature, these types of shows are designed to increase the viewer's beliefs and knowledge of certain dogma. These directly influence our self-perception. The more we are exposed to certain ideology, the more it will affect our beliefs about our self-worth. Television has certainly affected our perception and become a "significant other" to hundreds of thousands of people.

Peers: A peer can be defined as someone in the same general category as we are. Usually, this means that people are peers if they are of approximately the same age, economic, and social status. This can be extended to include people who are involved in the same professions or activities whether or not the other demographics are present. For example, all your classmates are your peers, to a certain extent, even though they are probably of various ages and backgrounds. Typically, peer influence (usually referred to as "peer pressure") has been associated with the teenage years. While it is certainly true that during the ages of 12-20 we often seem to be more preoccupied with how our friends accept or view something, peer pressure starts much younger and influences us throughout our lives.

Suppose Ashley is taking piano lessons while the rest of the neighborhood children are playing softball. When she is asked to play ball, she replies that she has to practice and can't play right now. The reaction of her peers will directly affect how she perceives herself. If they understand that playing the piano is a valuable tool, then she will view herself more positively, but if they respond negatively, her self-concept is apt to take a nosedive. Adults are certainly not immune to such pressure either. The phrase, "keeping up with the Joneses" was penned to refer to just such cases. We have a perfectly respectable car. It runs well and looks fairly good, but is ten years old. Suddenly, our neighbors and friends all seem to be purchasing new cars. When such an instance occurs, it is probably safe to assume that our self-concept may be affected (or our pocketbook will be) as we struggle to make car payments on a new vehicle. This is not to imply that everyone is equally affected by their peers and a desire to look good in their eyes, but to one extent or another most people tend to view themselves with the help of other's perception.

Society: The society in which we live affects our personal views. All societies have rules and regulations that its people are expected to observe. Some of these are written as laws and rules that govern our behaviors, but a great many of them aren't recorded anywhere, but are carefully followed just the same. These social norms are the unwritten laws that affect our self-concepts.

If we value the social norms of the society we live in, then we will try to comply with its rules, written and unwritten. The extent to which we feel we accomplish these goals will influence how we interpret our own behavior and self-esteem. For example, most people believe that there is something called "polite conversation." This usually refers to the choice of words and manner used when talking to people we respect or know only on a casual basis. If while talking to your minister, you slip and accidentally either use an "inappropriate" word or become angry, you will probably feel bad about the incident. In some way this will affect how you feel about yourself. You may think of yourself as being rude or become embarrassed by your behavior. If this type of incident occurs frequently, you may even begin to think of yourself as an unfeeling person and it could affect how you relate to others in general.

We view ourselves through the people we are involved with and this includes that vast array of humanity that we call society. How we fit into this society and perceive our relationship to it affects our self-concept just as other more specific relationships do. While the effect the general society has on our perspective may not be as clear as the effect your parents have

had, it exists and should be considered as you examine who, what and where you perceive yourself to be.

Now that you are familiar with the different categories that influence the self-concept, it is time to look specifically at your own self beliefs and see how you got them so you can begin to more fully understand yourself.

Self-Concept Exercise

This exercise will enable you to take a closer look at your self-perception and where these ideas originated.

1. Write a description of how you perceive yourself in each of the following categories:
   a. Physical Characteristics. (Do you see yourself as short, thin, blonde, muscular, etc.?)
   b. Relationships. (What relationships are you most involved in: spouse, children, sibling, friend?)
   c. Social Skills. (Are you outgoing, withdrawn, talkative?)
   d. Talents. (What are you good at, or would like to be: music, mechanics, swimming, speaking?)
   e. Strongly-held Beliefs. (Are you a pro-lifer, Christian, political activist?)
   f. Intellectual Ability. (Are you good at math, science, spelling, Spanish?)
2. After writing these descriptions, take a look at all you said. Are these statements really true? Are any of them obsolete? Write a summary of what you've learned.
3. As an addition to this assignment, you might like to have someone else you know fill out the questions about you and compare them with your answers.

While it is important to realize those people and things that have had an effect in helping you form your self-concept, it is extremely important to realize that it is _your_ self-concept. You and you alone are responsible for what you believe about yourself. Blaming mommy, daddy or society for how you feel or what you are, is merely an exercise in self-indulgence. By making others a scapegoat for your own responses, you are denying your responsibility. If there is something about yourself that you do not like, blaming someone else will not change it. Only you can make a better you.

The Nature of the Self-Concept

Before attempting to alter your self-concept, consider the following two principles that are the nature of the self-concept:

1. The self-concept is subjective.
2. A healthy self-concept must change, but resists change.

Let's take a look at each of the principles separately. "A self-concept is subjective" means that we do not see ourselves without bias. It is difficult to step outside of ourselves and form a factual opinion of the person we are viewing. When we are engaged in an argument, we find it difficult, if not impossible, to see where we may be wrong. We are too involved with self to be able to clearly monitor our behavior. In addition, we very often carry old perceptions of ourselves that are no longer true. For instance, I have always considered myself to be a poor mathematician; therefore, that's the label I put upon myself. A few years ago my best friend, after hearing my talk about how poor I was in math, said "Oh, really? Who is it that kept books for Holiday Inn, figures out several income tax forms, pays the bills, balances the checkbook, and figures her students' grades?" She had effectively shown me that while I might have been a poor mathematician at one time, I was no longer that person. It is obviously important that we take a self-inventory to see that our self-concept is up to date.

Not only do we deceive ourselves about our self-concepts, but others can distort our self-concept by incorrect feedback. Simply stated that means they lie to us. Distorted feedback can be either favorable or negative. It can be prompted by good or bad intentions, but nonetheless it helps us form an unrealistic self-concept. A secretary, with good intentions, may mislead her boss's perception of himself by constantly reinforcing her belief that he is an organized person, when in fact it is she who sees to the details of his everyday affairs. If he is told often enough that he is well organized, he will begin to believe it, even though it is untrue. A child who is constantly told he is a poor learner by those around him will begin to think of himself that way, even if he has a high IQ. These examples show us how our concepts can be distorted through others' feedback. The subjectivity of the self-concept is an important principle to keep in mind as you begin to evaluate your self-concept.

The second principle which states "a healthy self-concept must change, but resists change" means that people change from day to day and their self-concept must constantly be updated, yet it will be difficult to accept such change. This reluctance to accept changes in ourselves is a deterrent to making changes. We all have a tendency to hold on to the known. We are also all fearful of the unknown. Taking into account the last two

statements, we can see why change is so difficult. A friend of mine who dropped out of school at 15 because she was pregnant finds it difficult to believe that people who hold master's degrees would find her enjoyable company. What she has failed to see is that while she may lack certain education, she is not stupid. She has completed her GED, holds a respectable position at her place of employment, and often beats the rest of us in Trivial Pursuit. She has made the transition from pregnant dropout to efficient intelligent employee and friend. She has accomplished this over a period of time with subtle changes that she has not been aware of. Therefore, even though she has made a major change in herself, her self-esteem remains unchanged. If a person knows what it feels like to be rejected, even though she does not like that rejection, she may find it easier to live with than to try to change. If we try to make changes we may fear even worse results. It is easier to live with what we know than to take the risk involved in changing. To have a healthy up-to-date self-concept we must attempt to change, despite the fears involved.

Influences of the Self-Concept on Communication

How we perceive ourselves has a direct influence on how we communicate with ourselves and others. Take the following quiz to see what effects your self-concept may have on your communications skills.

Self-Concept Quiz

Answer the following questions by responding either A or B. Try to be honest by choosing what you usually do, not what you think you should do.

1. When first meeting people, I anticipate
   A. liking them until shown otherwise.
   B. disapproving of them until proven wrong.
2. When people first meet me, I expect them to
   A. accept and like me.
   B. reject and dislike me.
3. When I have completed a task, I think
   A. This is good; I've done my best.
   B. This could have been done better.
4. When I am doing something and someone is watching me I
   A. do better than I would have done if they weren't watching.
   B. do worse than I would have done if they weren't watching.
5. I work harder for people who
   A. demand high standards of me and can be critical of my work.
   B. expect less of me and are not very critical.
6. When I am around people I view as superior to me in some way, I feel
   A. comfortable and nonthreatened.
   B. uncomfortable and threatened.
7. When someone makes a negative remark about me, I react by being
   A. assertive and defend myself.
   B. passive and sometimes I even believe they're right.

If you answered the questions with a majority of "A" answers, congratulations! You probably have a positive healthy self-concept. If the answers are mostly "B's," chances are you tend to like yourself less and your lower self-esteem is affecting your communication in a negative way.

Self-Fulfilling Prophecies

A major influence on how we view ourselves is a phenomena known as the self-fulfilling prophecy. Self-fulfilling prophecy is defined as a strongly held belief which makes the outcome of an event more likely to happen: You wake up in the morning believing that it will be a wonderful day, so it is. You attend a party you know will be boring, so it is. You fail your math test even though you studied because you know you can't take tests well. A self-fulfilling prophecy can be either positive or negative. Although most of us realize we are capable of "psyching ourselves up" for a situation, we frequently fail to realize that the opposite is also true.

While it would be naive and inaccurate to believe that "thinking makes it so," belief in the outcome of something will certainly have its effect. If we think we can accomplish a task, we will at the very least attempt it. On the other hand, if we think we will fail, we may never initiate the project. If we build up numerous negative self-fulfilling prophecies, our self-concept will suffer. We may develop a low self-esteem, viewing ourselves as ineffectual and failures. Although believing in our capabilities will not assure success, it will enhance the outcome.

Self-fulfilling prophecies can either be self-imposed or imposed by outside forces. This means your belief may stem from something you hold to be true, or something others have told you. Consequently, when reviewing the effects of your self-fulfilling prophecies on your self-concept, it is necessary to evaluate the source of the information and judge its accuracy. Remember that self-imposed prophecies may not be objective and that prophecies imposed from outside may be distorted. Since I believed I was poor in math, I avoided figures. When I realized that information was false, I was free of the limits of my negative self-fulfilling prophecy. So it is with a person that has been told all his life that he is shy. After being told this for years, his behavior has reinforced the belief. He believes himself to be shy. If he reviews the self-fulfilling prophecy that has led him to this state and realizes that he was misled by others' comments, he can begin to erase the limits of their self-fulfilling prophecy.

The importance of self-fulfilling prophecies upon our self-concept is great. Whether they are positive or negative prophecies, self- or other-imposed, they affect our perception of ourselves. It is essential that you be aware of these effects as you begin the process of creating a more positive self-concept.

Exercise: Self-Fulfilling Prophecies

The following activity will help you more fully understand how your negative beliefs affect your self-concept.

1. List three negative self-fulfilling prophecies of yours. Word these statements as follows: "I *can't* quite smoking, lose weight, talk to people."

2. After completing step one, rewrite the statements using the words "I won't" instead of "I can't." (You may find this somewhat painful to accept, but in actuality it is probably closer to the truth. There are really very *few* things we *can't* do.)

3. Now decide the following about each prophecy.

   a. Was it self-imposed or imposed by outside forces?

   b. Does it fall into the category of "I can't," "I won't" or "I don't know how to"?

4. After making the previous decisions take some time to reflect on how these prophecies have kept you from achieving goals, living life to its fullest, or realizing your full potential. Write down these ideas and list some possible ways to overcome them.

Creating a Positive Self-Concept

After examining your self-concept you may have discovered certain areas in which you would like to make changes. If so, the following three points will help you accomplish your goal:

1. Make the change a priority in your life.
2. Develop the skills to make the change possible.
3. Stick to your decision to make the change.

By making the change a priority in your life you will, through a new self-fulfilling prophecy, make it more likely to occur. We are all busy people and have much to accomplish on a day-to-day basis. If changing your self-concept is not a high-priority item, you will find it difficult to maintain the energy and mindset required to bring about the change. It is important to realize that changing is difficult. By prioritizing the desired changes, you will have eliminated many complications that could distract you from your goal.

Having the skills to change requires that you first decide whether the desired change is one that you feel you can't change, you have not changed because you won't, or one which you don't know how to change. If it is truly one that you cannot change (due to physical limitations or other people involved), it is best to accept the fact and learn to live with it. If it is a case of something that in the past you wouldn't change (because you really didn't want to, or the change would require giving up something you chose not to lose), then you must again refer to the first guideline which is to make it a priority.

You must truly want to change. If you do not know how to make the change there are several steps you can take to educate yourself on the process. Bookstores and libraries contain numerous self-help manuals from stopping smoking to how to build a backyard deck. Read these or take a course in which you can learn the skills that you need. Observe people who display those traits you wish to develop or talk to an expert. Once you have mastered the skills, you will magically find that your self-concept has changed.

Involved in the process of developing skills you may find that you will have to remove yourself from negative influences. This may mean developing new relationships or changing your environment. This is a difficult part of the process, but essential to the successful completion of your goal. Seeking and developing new skills is time-consuming and often frustrating, but well worth the investment.

Having made the decision to make the change, you must follow through. Self-concepts are not formed quickly. They are the culmination of many years of interpretations. It is unrealistic to believe that any change will come quickly. Having the will to stick to your decision will carry you through the times when the desired change seems slow in coming. Depending upon the magnitude of the change, it could take years to achieve your goal. The best advice is to remember to approach it one day at a time. No one can face living on a low calorie diet the rest of her life, but we are all capable of controlling our appetite one day at a time. Be sure to seek out positive reinforcement from yourself and others. This will make it easier to persevere.

Knowing the formation and nature of the self-concept, its influences on communication and the effect of self-fulfilling prophecies will help you develop a more healthy, positive self-concept. The decision of whether or not you feel that a change is necessary is up to you. However, remember that the self-concept must be updated periodically. Whatever our self-perception, negative or positive, we all find it necessary to defend this image. The next section of the chapter will discuss the nature of this process.

Protecting Your Self-Concept: Defensiveness

Our self-concepts are by their very nature personal and yet on public display at the same time. Each of us has basically two selves that on occasion need to be defended. We have our "private self" (what we truly believe to be true about ourselves) and a "public self" (how we wish others to see us). While this is not meant to imply that we are all two-faced and our public and private images are diversely perceived, it does mean that there are those factors or beliefs that we know to be true personally, that we would rather not present to the general public, or even to those in our lives we consider to be close. Many of the concepts we hold true in our private perception and those we present to the world at large are the same. For example, I consider myself to be an honest person both privately and publicly. It is, however, those items that are contradictory in our perception and what we present to the world that often cause the largest and most intense displays of defensiveness. If I want my co-workers to see me as a responsible person, and yet know privately that I tend to shirk my duties and tasks if I can slide by, I will tend to become more defensive than if I truly believe I am a responsible person. It is as if the person accusing me of irresponsibility has seen through my facade and caught me in the act of betraying my public image.

Defensiveness can be defined as actions taken to protect the public image. It is one of the biggest barriers to communication that we face. The reason defensiveness is so detrimental to communication is because it is usually reciprocal. This means that when one person becomes defensive, the other person involved is likely to respond in a defensive manner as well. Once you have all participants trying to defend their self-concepts, the likelihood of any honest communication occurring is rather distant. Once we become involved in defending ourselves, we tend to be so consumed with this process that we fail to listen to the other person and communication goes out the window.

When you are in a position to protect yourself from a physical attacker, you can respond in one of two ways: You can either fight back or you can attempt to run away, fleeing the situation. The same two options are available when our self-concept is verbally attacked.

Mechanisms Used in Defensiveness

When we believe our public image has been attacked, we can choose to fight back (usually causing defensiveness in our partner) or we can try to run away (in a manner of speaking) from the attack. Let us consider these two general areas to see some of the specific actions that are often taken.

Fight: When we choose this option, we are usually trying to not only defend our self-concept, but to retaliate against the injury, and therefore the injurer, by giving some explanation as to why the accusation is untrue, or we try to turn the tables on the other person by pointing out some factor that he is deficient in. One of the ways this is done is through *rationalization*, giving a logical but essentially untrue explanation of why we did something: "I didn't call you like I said I would because the kids were sick." Another style is to *project* the offense on the accuser: "Sure the house is a mess, but I'm not responsible. You're the one who didn't do the dishes last night." When the situation seems too dangerous to fight back with the other person involved because of the relationship or power the other person may have, we can use *displacement* and fight with someone totally uninvolved in the defensive situation: Your boss tells you that you aren't doing your job right. You don't want to argue with the boss so you can go home and yell at your spouse. This type of behavior often sets off a chain of events that can lead to the youngest child in the family kicking the dog. If all else fails, we can always resort to being *verbally aggressive,* raising our voice, yelling accusations, calling names and hope that he who yells loudest or gets nastiest will win by overpowering his opponent with loud, insulting verbiage.

Flee: When we choose to run away as a means of defense, we have several options available to us. We may try to *compensate* for a defect by changing the subject or bringing up an area we are good in; "Yeah, well 'I may have flunked math, but I got an 'A' in English." We may react as if nothing has happened and use *apathy,* or react just the opposite of how we are truly feeling; "Ok, so he stood me up. Big deal! I don't care." We may retreat to a *fantasy* where we are in control, or try to convince ourselves that what we have been accused of isn't true about us. We may offer weak excuses for our actions by retorting that it's not that we meant to let the car run out of oil, causing hundreds of dollars worth of damage, it's just that we didn't know how to add it. Rather than admit we failed to do something, or did something we shouldn't have, we can try to *undo* the perception by sending flowers, making his favorite dinner, or buying the kids that toy they've been begging for. Finally, we can try to totally *repress* the situation or action by disavowing any connection to it; "You must be mistaken about that; my child would never steal!"

All of these actions are common ways in which we try to protect our public image. The method (or combination of methods) we use depends upon the person who is defensive, the relationship of the people involved, and the environment of the situation. Chances are that these methods are not unfamiliar to you. You probably can remember times you have acted in just such a fashion. Defensive behavior is not necessarily negative or bad; it can serve a beneficial function by doing what it is meant to do: protect us. But when defensiveness is involved, effective communication will probably not take place; and when we flee or fight we aren't really doing anything about the cause of the problem, just merely defending it. If communication and solving the problem are important, then becoming defensive will only complicate the issue. There are ways to limit the possibility of creating the on-going spiral of defensiveness that can help you improve upon these situations.

Methods of Limiting and Overcoming Defensiveness

Psychologist Jack Gibb* has categorized defense producing behaviors (those actions that lead to people becoming defensive) into six categories

*From: *Looking Out, Looking In, 4/e,* by Ronald B. Adler & Neil Towne. Copyright © 1984 by CBS College Publishing. Copyright © 1981, 1978 by Holt, Rinehart & Winston. Copyright © 1975 by Rinehart Press. Reprinted by permission of CBS College Publishing.

and countered them with supportive behaviors that tend to lessen the likelihood of defensiveness occurring.

Gibb Categories

Defensive Behaviors	*Supportive Behaviors*
1. evaluation	1. description
2. control	2. problem orientation
3. strategy	3. spontaneity
4. neutrality	4. empathy
5. superiority	5. equality
6. certainty	6. provisionalism

Before describing each of these categories, it is important that you know just how they work and can be used in general. Whenever the defensive behaviors are used, the likelihood of the people involved becoming defensive is increased. In fact, it is almost a certainty that when these behaviors are engaged in, someone will become defensive. On the other hand, when the supportive behaviors are used, the chance of defensiveness occurring is decreased (remember, though, that it is less of a certainty because we have no control over the actions of others; if they wish to become defensive, they will). The supportive behaviors can be used in two ways. If you normally respond to circumstances in one of the defense-producing ways, you can learn how to implement the supportive behavior, therefore keeping the environment freer of defensive reactions. Another possibility is when someone else has said something that you interpret as defensive to you, instead of responding with a defensive mechanism, you can respond in one of the supportive behaviors, lessening the possibility of a reciprocal mechanism from the other person. The supportive behaviors leave the channels of effective communication open, increasing the chance of resolving the difficulty.

Now, let's look at each of the categories and see what they can accomplish.

Evaluation/Description:

When we *evaluate* someone or something, we pass judgment. We say it is "right," "wrong," "stupid," "intelligent," "messy," or "clean." Even if we are in a position to have the authority to do this, we still tend to create defensive behaviors in the person being evaluated. In this method we use a lot of "you" language. "You should have done better; you never listen to me; you're lazy." When we use these types of statements, we are not only making inferences to people's actions and character, but we are also stating them as facts.

The supportive behavior of *description* allows us to state our thoughts and feelings for what they are, our opinion. It is less defense-producing to say that a certain action on the part of another affects us a certain way by relating it using "I" language. "I believe you could have done better; when you ignore what I say, I feel upset because I think you don't love me; I think you're shirking your responsibilities and I'm left with more work." While these comments essentially express the same ideas as the "you" language statements, the approach is much less defense-producing.

Control/Problem Orientation:

Anytime we attempt to *control* a situation, we create a defensive climate. When we try to be the boss and tell people what to do, we not only negate their abilities, but also take their desire to accomplish the goal. Furthermore, we place ourselves in a position of authority that even when we have the right to do so, often causes feelings of defensiveness. When we use the supportive behavior of *problem orientation* instead, we take into account the other person's feelings and ideas making them a part of the solution.

Problem orientation is a process that involves cooperation. When a problem is seen to exist, all parties sit down and define what they perceive the problem to be and try to reach a mutual consensus on how to solve the conflict. This takes time, but in the long run will work better than control which is not only defense-producing, but must be exerted time and time again.

Strategy/Spontaneity:

When we use *strategy,* we are trying to manipulate the other person involved to do something we want done. This may achieve your goal of getting to the movie on Saturday night when your transportation is out of commission, but the chances of the person you manipulated being a charming and fun companion are slim. She will more likely be angry and defensive because she has been tricked into doing something.

Spontaneity, the supportive behavior, is simply being honest with the other person. When we are honest, come right out and ask for a favor, the other person involved has the right to make up her own mind without pressure. While you may find that using spontaneity doesn't result in your immediate desires being met as often as being manipulative, you will find that allowing others to be a part of the decision-making process will result in more pleasant outcomes for all involved.

Neutrality/Empathy:

Neutrality is ignoring other people. When we fail to respond to someone who is obviously trying to engage us in conversation (even if we do so unintentionally), we will be creating a defensive climate. The reason for this is obvious; who likes to feel as if he isn't important enough to be listened to? I come home from school and want to discuss something that happened in class with my husband, and he merely turns up the sound on the TV. I'm sure to become defensive and probably angry with him. On the other hand, if he treats me with the supportive behavior of *empathy*, listening to what I have to say, I will be less likely to become upset even if his response is, "I think you're over-reacting." When we use empathy, trying to listen and really understand the verbals and non-verbals, we are showing them that we care about them.

Superiority/Equality:

Acting better than someone else by showing *superiority* is a sure-fire way to cause defensiveness. Just because we have an edge in position or relationship doesn't mean that they are less of a human being than we are. If I, as a teacher treat my students with superiority because I'm the *teacher*, I will most assuredly set myself up with a hostile class that will learn very little.

The supportive behavior of *equality* is much more likely to produce positive results. Treating others with equality does not negate the fact that some people have more knowledge or skill at certain things than others. My students are perfectly willing to concede that I probably know more about effective communication than they do, but that doesn't mean that I am better than they are. We are all human beings who possess abilities that, while different, are not necessarily unequal.

Certainty/Provisionalism:

If you know someone who always acts as if they are right, no matter what proof you give, then you are familiar with the defense-producing behavior of *certainty*. It is fairly simple to see why we react in a defensive manner when someone fails to even consider what we have to say. They are right and that's final!

Provisionalism, the supportive behavior, can be used to lessen the defensiveness by allowing the other person to state his beliefs, reasons and feelings. Even if these thoughts can't be incorporated into the picture, the mere fact that he has been allowed to state them will make the atmosphere less hostile and solutions are more readily accepted.

Defensiveness is a normal, predictable behavior to comments or situations that attack our self-concepts. Everyone has at one time or another experienced this emptional state. Defensiveness is not bad nor is it necessarily undesirable, but remember that for communication to survive, the defensiveness must be kept at a low level or the chances of a mutually satisfactory outcome are almost nil.

Conclusion

Our self-concepts are what make up our very essence as human beings. How we think and feel about ourselves affects not only our lives and accomplishments, but our communication and relationships with others. When we try to protect these images by becoming defensive, we create an environment that is detrimental to ourselves, others and the survival of communication.

Bibliography

Langer, Ellen J. and Carol S. Dweck. Personal Politics: *The Psychology of Making It.* Englewood Cliffs, NJ: Prentice-Hall, Inc., 1973.

Powell, Barbara. *Overcoming Shyness.* New York: McGraw-Hill Company, 1979.

Rubin, Theodore I. *Compassion and Self-Hate.* New York: David McKay Co., 1975.

Schultz, Duane, *Growth Psychology: Models of the Healthy Personality.* New York: Van Nostrand Reinhold Company, 1977.

Shostram, Everett L. *Freedom to Be.* Englewood Cliffs, NJ: Prentice-Hall, Inc. 1972.

Smith, Manuel J. *Kicking the Fear Habit.* New York: Dial Press, 1977.

Zimbardo, Philip G. *Shyness: What It Is. What To Do About It.* Reading, Mass: Addison-Wesley Publishing Co., 1977.

3

Self-Disclosure: Thoughts and Feelings

I. We can let others know us through self-disclosure.

   A. The Johari Window presents a picture of us.

   B. This window shows potential for communication.

II. There are at least two benefits of self-disclosure.

   A. Relationships grow.

   B. Our health improves.

III. We present five suggestions to facilitate self-disclosure.

   A. Express your emotions for the purpose of communicating.

   B. Keep your disclosure centered on the present.

   C. Consider the environment of the disclosure.

   D. Try to send efficient messages.

   E. Don't judge your emotions.

Introduction

> When a man discloses his experience
> to another, fully, spontaneously, and
> honestly, then the mystery that he
> was decreases enormously.
>
> From *The Transparent Self*
> By Sindney M. Jourard

Have you even thought of yourself as a mystery? A mystery so great and vast that even Miss Marple and Sherlock Holmes couldn't unravel it? You are. Everyone is. But it doesn't take a team of the world's greatest detectives to solve that mystery; you and only you can reveal yourself to others solving that mystery. When you open up and honestly reveal your thoughts and feelings to another human being, you are sharing the greatest gift you have to give. A gift unlike any other, one that can never be duplicated or copied, but that can enrich your life and the lives of those around you.

Self-disclosure is the act of deliberately revealing your thoughts and feelings as they occur. It deals in the "here and now" and allows the people involved to get to know you for what you are, a human being full of wonderful ideas, opinions, contradictory feelings and expectations that make the human species so unique and marvelous. When we open up to another person, we are willing to risk the possible complications and possible consequences that say, "Here I am; this is who and what I am." Many of us fear such disclosure for numerous reasons and because of these fears limit our potential to be fully understood and known by others. Obviously, there are risks involved in sharing yourself with others, but the benefits far outweigh the chances you take when self-disclosure allows you to share the very essence that makes you *you*.

A Model of Self: The Johari Window*

Joseph Luft and Harry Ingham have created the following model that can help us examine our own potential for self-disclosure. As you peruse this part of the chapter, become familiar with the four quadrants that comprise each of us and try to imagine what your own personal Johari Window might look like.

Pretend that you have a window that will allow you to look inside and see everything there is about yourself.

```
+---------------------------+
|                           |
|                           |
|                           |
|                           |
|        Everything         |
|          about            |
|           you             |
|                           |
|                           |
|                           |
|                           |
+---------------------------+
```

Now, since we aren't completely aware of everything we are, divide that window into two parts (vertically). These sections will represent the area you are aware of, *known to self,* and the other represents the area you are unaware of, *not known to self.*

```
+-------------+-------------+
|             |             |
|             |     Not     |
|    Known    |    known    |
|      to     |      to     |
|     self    |     self    |
|             |             |
|             |             |
+-------------+-------------+
```

*From: *Looking Out, Looking In, 4/e,* by Ronald B. Adler & Neil Towne. Copyright © 1984 by CBS College Publishing. Copyright © 1981, 1978 by Holt, Rinehart & Winston. Copyright © 1975 by Rinehart Press. Reprinted by permission of CBS College Publishing.

Since even the least disclosing person, is known at least partially to other people, we can also divide the window into two other sections (horizontally): those things that *others know about us* and those things that are *unknown to others.*

```
┌─────────────────────────┐
│                         │
│        Known            │
│       to others         │
│                         │
├─────────────────────────┤
│                         │
│       Not known         │
│       to others         │
│                         │
└─────────────────────────┘
```

Now, let's superimpose these last two windows on top of each other, and you can see that everything about you can be divided into four basic quadrants that will allow you to examine yourself and your self-disclosure more clearly.

```
┌────────────┬────────────┐
│     1      │     2      │
│            │            │
│   OPEN     │   BLIND    │
├────────────┼────────────┤
│     3      │     4      │
│            │            │
│  HIDDEN    │  UNKNOWN   │
└────────────┴────────────┘
```

The area that you and others are aware of is labelled the *open* quadrant. This is the area that you share through active self-disclosure or obvious actions and comments that others can easily interpret. This is the area of interpersonal communication and thus the area where self-disclosure takes place.

The *hidden* area makes up that part of you that you are aware of, but others don't know about. These may be parts of yourself that you fear to disclose to others because you believe they would be injurious to you in some way, things that you are willing to disclose but haven't had the time or opportunity to share, or thoughts and feelings that do not need to be disclosed to others.

The *blind* area is known to others, but not to yourself. It is comprised of those aspects of your personality or actions that others are fully aware of about you, but which you don't comprehend.

The final quadrant is labelled *unknown* because it is the area of self that neither you nor others are aware of. This can be considered a store house of things that have yet to come to light, or may be thought of as the area of potential growth.

Now take a moment to think about your own self-disclosure in general. How do you perceive yourself? Do you believe that you are fairly open and sharing and therefore would have a fairly large *open* quadrant? Do you see yourself with a lot of hidden secrets and pent up emotions that you rarely share? If so, you may have a rather large *hidden* area. Do you believe others know more about you than you yourself are aware of which makes a large *blind* quadrant? The *unknown* area can be considered as always there and the size may not be of much importance, but if you believe that you not only have a lot to learn about yourself, but that others hardly know you either, you might consider the *unknown* area to be fairly significant.

It is fairly reasonable to suggest that not only does each person have a unique and different Johari Window, but that an individual's window will probably vary from situation to situation and according to whom he is with. Obviously most of us feel more comfortable opening up to someone we feel close to. While we may consider ourselves fairly closed in general, with our closer friends we may indeed have a larger open area. By estimating our own personal Johari Window we can get an idea of the percentage of ourselves that we tend to self-disclose.

While the Johari Window is a model of one person's self-disclosure, we can use it to see how self-disclosure works as two people attempt to have a discussion. Look at the two models that follow. Pretend that one model is John's and one model represents Jane.

Conversation will probably flow fairly smoothly only as long as John's and Jane's open areas are equal in size. What will happen when John (the more open of the two) attempts to share more than Jane is willing to disclose? Let's look at the possibilities: John might open up sections that Jane will fear to share and an argument might ensue; John might monopolize the conversation and turn it into a monologue leaving Jane to listen or ignore him as she pleases; John may recognize Jane's reluctance to share any further and retreat to "safer" subjects; or Jane might open up more and share some of her thoughts and feelings with John, thus

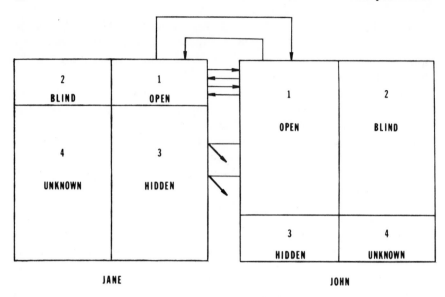

JANE   JOHN

increasing the size of her own open area. Which do you think is most likely
to happen? If you chose the latter, (Jane opening up more) then you would
be correct in over 50% of the time. Most people will reciprocate when
someone shares with them. They probably won't be willing to share as much
of their thoughts and feelings as the person who initiates the disclosure, but
they probably will share more than if left to begin the disclosure themselves.
The reason for this is that self-disclosure involves trust and trust is usually
reciprocal. If I trust you enough to share my feelings about something with
you, you will be more likely to share with me; maybe you won't share at the
exact same level or as much, but over 50% of the time you will respond with
some form of disclosure.

A significant person in my life used to be fairly closed. He would rarely
share his emotions with me, particularly if he considered them negative
ones. If we disagreed about something, we never argued because rather than
expose his feelings, he would simply leave, usually with a forced smile on his
face. Now, I could have ended the relationship because I believed that we
would never really have a strong relationship without open communication,
but instead I kept expressing my feelings even as he walked out the door.
One evening he started to leave and I noticed that he slammed the door and
I had to smile (even though I was angry) because I realized that he was

finally beginning to disclose, at least non-verbally. After several months he began to share his emotions more and open up. It took time, energy and a lot of work on both our parts, but it was worth it. Self-disclosure is not only important, but is essential for several reasons.

The Benefits of Self-Disclosure

Due to the risks (real and perceived) involved in self-disclosure it is no wonder that many people fear to share their thoughts and feelings with others. However, the benefits of self-disclosure are so great and rewarding that they far outweigh the risks. As Bernard Gunther says, "Take a chance on getting slapped; you might get kissed."

While there are numerous advantages to sharing what you think and feel, we will look at the two general benefits that incorporate most of these.

Relationships grow when mutual self-disclosure is incorporated into the partnership. Whether you refer to a marriage, parent/child, friends, employer/employee, or any other relationship, the growth and strength of

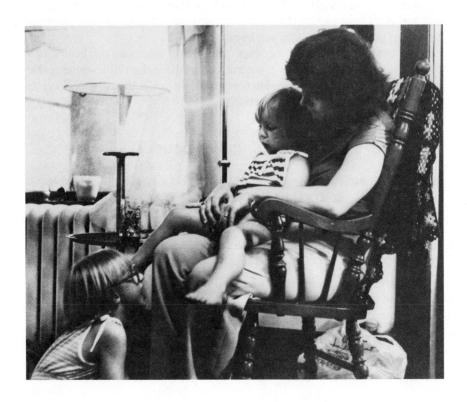

that interaction is directly related to the quality and amount of self-disclosure within that relationship. There are many reasons for this, including the obvious one that there is greater understanding of each person involved and this greater understanding leads to less emotional stress and argument. Further more, we increase our own self esteem when we share what we truly feel and believe. As self esteem grows, we improve our self concepts. The healthier and more positive a self concept a person has, the more he can help others realize their potential, and this in turn often leads to increased and stronger communication between people. We have already stated that trust is reciprocal. Self-disclosure is based upon trust and trust is an ingredient in strong relationships.

Your health improves when you share your emotions. As you disclose to others, you will be sharing your feelings as well as your thoughts. Studies have shown that repressing (i.e., not sharing) your emotions can lead to illness. When we fail to let people know how we feel and keep it bottled up inside of us, we cause stress to increase. Stress works on the immunological system causing it to function less actively which means we are more likely to become ill. Ulcers, headaches, back pain, hypertension, cardiovascular problems, and many other physical health problems have been linked to the non-self-disclosing personality. Clearly if we learn to open up and share our emotions, our physical health will improve.

With the over-powering evidence that exists that self-disclosure is a positive force in relationships and health benefits, it should be obvious that this is a skill that will help you survive. Next we'll investigate ways to increase your ability to implement this process.

Facilitating Disclosure

There are many reasons that we fail to self-disclose, but one of the biggest problems we face in improving this skill is the fact that rarely have we been taught how and what to do to increase this sharing ability that we all possess. The following section is designed to answer some of the questions you may have and give you some ideas that will help increase the effectiveness of your communication.

1. *Express your emotions and thoughts to communicate*, not to manipulate or ventilate. When we tell another how we feel or what we think, we must remember that they are our *own* beliefs; this does not make them facts. The most effective means of sharing these thoughts is to take ownership for them and not blame others for what we think or feel. It is effective self-disclosure to state, "I feel sad," it is not effective to say,

"You made me feel sad." Our emotions evolve from our interpretations of sense data, not from the sense data itself. Pretend that you have never fallen down the stairs and don't know that it can be a painful and dangerous situation. You are witness to someone falling down a flight of stairs. What is your reaction? Chances are you might be amused. It looks funny and you might even laugh aloud. Now, knowing what you really know about the situation, what is your reaction to the same episode? Fear, concern, worry? The difference in these examples is not one of sense data, what happened, but rather how you interpreted the situation that caused the change in emotion. Therefore, who is responsible for your feelings? You. Intellectually, most of us can accept this, but it becomes harder when we truly believe that the other person caused us to respond. What is at work here is the idea that if we feel a certain way, the other person meant us to feel that way. She knows I get angry when supper is late, hence, she wanted me to become angry. The validity of this type of thinking can quickly be disputed if we look at it in a few other ways. If people can *make* you feel a certain way, then logically you should be able to get others to feel the way you want them to and we all know this isn't true. You can't make someone love you. Another way to test the belief is to take the presumption that if people can make us feel, then they should be able to make us feel happy when we are depressed, upset or down in the dumps. If this were true, wouldn't we always be in a good mood? Obviously, we must be responsible for how we feel. When disclosing our thoughts and feelings, it is important to remember that we are relating only our interpretations and perceptions and must not infer that others are causing it. This will not only be the truth, but will cut down on the likelihood of our setting up a defensive climate that is unhealthy to communication.

2. *Keep your disclosure centered on the present*; do not bring up old gripes. When you disclose, it is a good idea to refrain from bringing up situations that are in the past. Last night's late arrival from a date doesn't belong in a discussion where you're relating your thoughts and feelings about today's dirty dishes. The exception to this is when all the referrals to the past have a direct influence on the present; such as all showing carelessness or lack of concern for others. When we suddenly bring up ideas and emotions that are not directly related to the topic at hand, we cloud the issue and decrease the effectiveness of the disclosure. Here is a comparison that will help you better understand this idea called "saving stamps." You are all probably familiar with commercial stamp saving like Eagle or Top Value stamps where you receive little coupons for the amount of merchandise purchased. These are then pasted into savings books and when the book(s) is filled, it entitles you to cash it in for prizes. Many of us "save stamps" with our emotions and thoughts. We save them up until we have a

full book and then we cash them in! We may cash them in by yelling and screaming, leaving home, going shopping or a million other ways, but cash them in we do. To those around us who are witnessing this outbreak of emotion it may very well seem that we are over-reacting to a small insignificant item. They don't know about the other 99 reactions that have helped fill the book because we have failed to disclose them as they occurred. We have merely grumbled to ourselves and stuck them in the book. They believe that a simple act of finding the dirty socks next to the hamper (instead of in the hamper) has set us off on a tirade. Yet we know that it isn't *just* the socks, but all the other instances (related or not) that we have saved up.

Remember to keep your disclosures related to the present and you will find that they will be easier for the other person to relate to. This facilitates understanding which will in turn increase the communication shared.

3. *Consider the environment of the disclosure* by taking into account the best time and place for the disclosure (As Chapter I states: "Environment" refers to the individual's point of view made up of her background, language, culture, experience—all the things that make the individual unique."). While it is usually good to express what you are feeling at the time it occurs, it is not always the right time and place to discuss it. During the initial reactions to situations and in the throes of strong emotions we may not be able to effectively express what we want to say. Also, consider what the other person is displaying—are they ready, in the right mood to listen to what you have to say? While it is not wise to postpone disclosures for too long, there are times when disclosure discussions are best served when all involved are most likely to reciprocate and listen to each other. However, there are those who choose to never find the right time and place and must be faced with your disclosures even if they aren't in the best environment at the time.

This guideline also refers to being aware of when it is necessary to self-disclose and when it will serve little or no purpose. If while on vacation in a strange city the taxi driver is rather rude, it would probably not be advantageous to express your thoughts or feelings on the matter. However, if you often ride with the same driver, you should tell her what you are thinking because it is appropriate to the relationship and environment.

There are no clear cut rules to alert you to when to disclose and when to refrain. You must try to gauge each instance as it presents itself. Remember that it is almost always a good idea to state your reaction (emotion and thought) as it occurs whether the time is right to delve deeper or not. Most of us tend to be on the cautious side and refrain from disclosing more often then we open up so we need to be more willing to take the risk. While we are not advocating opening yourself up to an obvious harm, we could almost all be a little more daring in our disclosures. Just judge the environment. Take a deep breath, and plunge in.

4. *Try to send efficient messages* that the other person can understand. (Refer to Chapter One on how to send efficient messages). While this doesn't mean that every time you open your mouth to speak you must include all four parts of sending an efficient message, it is important to send as clear a message as possible. Don't just relate your interpretation and leave out your reaction to it. After all, it is your reaction, belief and/or emotion, that is necessary for the other person to know if they are to understand what you are saying. Choose your words carefully. Try to be clear and concise, to the point. Use language that is shared in connotative meaning by both of you and remember to express it in a non-defensive manner. By keeping these ideas in mind and practicing your disclosure skills, you will find that your communication and relationships will be improved. This will affect your life in a positive way.

5. *Don't judge your emotions;* they aren't *"good"* or *"bad"*, they just are. Labelling your feelings negative or positive will only add complications to the disclosing process. If you think that love is good and hate is bad, you will shy away from expressing those emotions you think are negative. In addition, when you experience what you consider "bad feelings" you will probably cause yourself to experience guilt and layer this emotion on top of the primary emotion making them harder to clearly self-disclose. Human beings experience a whole range of emotions and they are neither good or bad. While we can judge actions that people take in response to such emotions, judging the emotions themselves is counter-productive to communication.

Diary of Awareness Exercise

Try the following exercise to acquaint you with how you handle self-disclosure.

1. For three days keep track of the predominate emotions that you experience. It is best if you take a few seconds several times a day to jot down a note about the experience rather than wait until evening to try and recall them.

2. State the emotion. Were you feeling happy, despondent, worried etc.?

3. Describe the situation that was occurring by stating the activating event(s), who was involved, and any other significant effects.

4. Discuss how you handled the emotion. Did you disclose it to another person verbally or non-verbally? Did you place it in

the hidden part of your Johari Window? If you disclosed it, tell how and record the reaction of any one else involved.

5. After three days write a summary of what you have learned about your disclosing behaviors.

Conclusion

Yes, there are risks involved in self-disclosure, but if you will think of your thoughts and feelings as serving the same purpose as fuses and circuit breakers in an electrical system, you will be able to see how vitally important sharing them is. Fuses and circuit breakers are incorporated into the electrical design to alert you to possible overloads that can lead to fires and injuries. Our emotions and beliefs serve the same purpose in our lives and relationships. Just as fuses set off an alarm before danger begins, so it is with those things we think and feel. No relationship has ever ended without some emotion or thought to warn us, and no one has ever committed suicide or had a nervous breakdown without something being perceived first. Our thoughts and feelings when disclosed alert all involved to what is happening. Self-disclosure is indeed a survival skill.

Bibliography

Bridges not Walls. 3rd Ed.   Ed. by John Stewart. Reading, Mass: Addison-Wesley Publishing Co., 1982.

Dahms, Allan M. *Emotional Intimacy: Overlooked Requirement for Survival.* Boulder, CO: Pruett Publishing Company, 1972.

Derlega, Valerian and Allan L. Schikin. *Sharing Intimacy.* Englewood Cliffs, NJ: Prentice-Hall, Inc., 1975.

Dyer, Wayne W. *Your Erroneous Zones.* New York: Avon, 1977.

Goldberg, Herbert. *The Hazards of Being Male: Surviving the Myth of Masculine Privilege.* Los Angeles: Nash, 1976.

Fromm, Erich. *The Art of Loving.* New York: Harper and Row Publishers, 1956.

Jourart, Sidney M. *The Transparent Self.* Princeton, NJ: D. Van Nostrand Company, Inc., 1964.

Powell, John S. J. *Why Am I Afraid to Tell You Who I Am?* Niles, Illinois: Argus Communications, 1969.

Tavris, Carol. *Anger: The Misunderstood Emotion.* New York: Simon and Schuster, 1983.

4

Listening

I. There is a difference between listening and hearing..
   A. Hearing is perceiving sounds.
   B. Listening is the willingness to understand.

II. The effects of nonlistening.
   A. It affects your mental abilities.
   B. It can result in misunderstandings.
   C. You may miss opportunities.
   D. It is costly.
   E. It promotes interpersonal conflicts.
   F. It hinders self-disclosure.
   G. It can result in defensiveness.

III. The benefits of listening.
   A. It will increase your maturity.
   B. It will improve your job success.
   C. It will improve your relationships.
   D. It will help protect you.

IV. Reasons we don't listen.
   A. We think talk is power and listening is passive.
   B. We tend to not listen unless we are entertained.
   C. We have assumptions and biases.
   D. We have distractions.
   E. We are often preoccupied.
   F. We may fear the material presented.
   G. We experience message-overload.
   H. The "speaking/thinking" rate may affect our listening.
   I. We are not taught to listen.

V. There are seven nonlistening styles.
   A. Pseudolistening.
   B. Stagehogging.
   C. Selective listening.
   D. Insulated listening.
   E. Defensive listening.
   F. Ambushing.
   G. Insensitive listening.

VI. A practical approach to listening improvement.

  A. Recognition.
  B. Refusal.
  C. Replacement.

VII. Typical ways of responding.

  A. Advising.
  B. Judging.
  C. Analyzing.
  D. Questioning.
  E. Supporting.

VIII. Active listening.

  A. Used when a problem is present.
  B. Used when there is undivided attention.
  C. Used when there is genuine concern for the partner.
  D. Used when you can withhold judgments and comments.

Definitions and Effects on Communication

"I can't hear you!"

"You never listen."

"Listen to me!"

"I know you heard me, but did you listen to me?"

Do any of these phrases sound familiar? Chances are they do. Most of us are receivers of such messages almost daily. Listening is an important factor in our lives. It is also one of the most neglected skills.

A good way to begin our study of listening is to understand the difference between "listening" and "hearing."

Hearing: The process of perceiving sound: the reverberation of sound waves in the ear.

Listening: The ability to pay attention: the willingness to understand oral communication.

By using these definitions it should be clear that listening and hearing are two different functions. Hearing is the physical act. Listening is an attempt to understand what you heard. Obviously, you cannot listen to something you haven't heard: but you *hear* many things you don't *listen* to.

Effects of Nonlistening

The effects that result from failure to listen are too numerous to be contained in a comprehensive list. However, by examining some general results we can see that nonlistening is a dangerous pastime. When we fail to listen to what we hear, we miss information. The loss of this data can result in several problems.

Probably the most obvious complication to nonlistening is the effect it has on the development of our *mental abilities.* Studies have shown that the average person spends at least 70% of each day involved in some form of communication (Nichols and Stevens, 1957, p. 6). Furthermore, approximately 55% of that time is spent in situations requiring listening

(Werner, 1975). Poor listening habits will decrease the amount of information we process, thus cutting down on our learning capabilities. Put very simply, this means that if you can't use information because you didn't listen, then you can't learn it. Poor listeners are less intelligent than good listeners because they have eliminated a large percent of the sources they could learn from.

Another problem that results from ineffective listening is *misunderstanding*. Misunderstanding means that something has been interpreted incorrectly. For example, you buy the wrong brand of dog food because you didn't listen when your mother told you to use the coupon to make your purchase; or your child gets and eats a cookie ten minutes before dinner because you didn't listen to what she said and simply nodded and said "Sure," so you could finish fixing supper without being interrupted. Misunderstandings also cause patients to receive the wrong medicine, and pilots to make mistakes due to misinterpreting orders from the control tower (Floyd, 9). Nonlistening that results in misunderstandings can range from mildly annoying to deadly.

A third effect of negligent listening is an abundance of *missed opportunities*. When we fail to listen to what others have to say, we run a great risk of losing out on a chance to go, do, or be involved in something. These opportunities may be small, relatively unimportant pastimes, or major investments that lead to high financial ventures.

The cost of ineffective listening can even be measured economically. Poor listening habits are *costly*. Sperry Corporation studied the listening habits of its employees and concluded that "with more than 100 million workers in

Non-listening can cause harm.

America, a simple ten dollar listening mistake by each of them would cost a billion dollars'' (p. 8). Often "letters have to be retyped; appointments rescheduled; shipments reshipped" (p. 8). The conclusion of the Sperry study states the distortion of ideas that is accompanied through people's failure to listen to each other is as high as "80% (distortion) as they travel through the chain of command" (p. 8). Not listening can lead to a loss of big bucks!

The effects of poor listening habits can also lead to *interpersonal conflicts*. Problems between people can often be traced back to failure to listen on one or several people's part. These are the times we fail to get the whole message or assume that we know what is being said and tune out. Other conflicts arise causing arguments, repression, or hurt feelings. All because we failed to listen to the other person.

Lack of self-disclosure is often a result of poor listening. Self-disclosure is based upon reciprocal trust and trust is developed when people perceive that others care. One of the signs of caring is a willingness to listen to others. Therefore, failure to listen will destroy the atmosphere needed to self-disclose. Without self-disclosure, relationships stagnate, communication deteriorates, and personal problems multiply.

Another effect caused by ineffective listening is *defensiveness*. One of the major causes of defensive behavior is "neutrality" exhibited by the partner: the belief that you are being ignored because your partner is reacting to you with a mask of apathy. Since defensiveness is reciprocal, it stands to reason that once one person becomes defensive, the other person will become defensive and listening flies out the window.

There are many other complications that are directly related to poor listening habits. All of them adversely affect communication which causes problems and wastes time. Luckily the reverse is also true. As listening behaviors improve, communication improves and the benefits of listening are as positive as the effects of poor listening are negative.

Benefits of Listening

Listening increases your *knowledge*. Since we learn by using our senses and hearing is one of those senses, it stands to reason that the more we use what we hear by listening, the more we increase our understanding and knowledge. Listening is the one communication skill we use the most. Over half of our daily communication time each day is spent listening. That is more time than we spend speaking, reading, and writing combined.

The increase in time spent listening to television and radio that has occurred over the past 15-20 years and the decreased time spent reading is further proof that more of our information is coming to us through listening. In fact, it has been discovered "that children who watch television are better listeners than those who do not" (p. 4). Further proof that listening is necessary for increasing knowledge can be found in the percentage of time that students are asked to devote to this skill. 60-70% of all classroom time is spent in listening activities. Obviously, a student who is an effective listener will learn more than one who is not.

A second benefit derived from listening improvement is increased *maturity*. Our society places a great deal of emphasis on the ability to handle ourselves and situations in a mature manner; yet it, like listening, is a skill that is seldom taught. Listening and maturity are directly related skills: a good listener is more mature than a poor listener. You will also find that a person who is perceived as possessing maturity is also a good listener. Let's take a look at why this is true.

While it is difficult to actually define all the ingredients that make up a "mature" attitude, one major factor is certainly that of patience. The ability to work, wait, and allow things to develop in their own way, at their own speed can only be achieved through application of this behavior. Those who possess this quality have learned it through trial, error, and time. These are mature individuals.

Listening, too, requires patience. One cannot rush the process. While we are capable of thinking approximately three to four times faster than most people speak, we are usually incapable of speeding up the speaker. In

addition to this fact, we must consider why the speaker is speaking. Very often we are in positions where the person speaking is doing so not necessarily to provide factual information, but to explain emotions. This takes time. Learning the virtue of patience will directly benefit the listening skill and provide a measure of maturity.

Perhaps a more obvious reward for listening is *job success.* Numerous surveys of employers and managers over the past five years have overwhelmingly rated listening as the number one communication skill necessary for successful employment (5-6). Obviously, the ability to listen well will improve your job skills, increase your chances at employment, lead to promotions, and add to economic security.

The fourth benefit of listening is *improved interpersonal relations.* Just as poor listening skills lead to problems between people, good listening helps improve and deepen relationships. You need no surveys or studies to prove this point. All you have to do is think about the last time someone really listened to you. He didn't interrupt with his own opinions; his comments showed he understood not only what you said, but how you said it. He may not have necessarily agreed with you, but he listened, and it felt good. Need a boost to a relationship? Try listening more to the other person. He'll probably reciprocate.

The last benefit that we will discuss is that of *self-protection.* The obvious interpretation of this benefit is that the better we become at listening, the less likely we are to miss information that will keep us from making mistakes that could harm us. For example, "The burner is hot; don't touch it!" The real benefits go much deeper than that and have great values particularly for people who live in free and democratic societies. The United States guarantees the freedom of speech in its constitution. Therefore many statements we hear, because our government allows our freedom of speech, are not necessarily true or to our advantage to believe. Freedom to speak as we desire is a wonderful right not shared by all the world's inhabitants; with it goes the responsibility to critically listen and analyze what is said. Protection from people who misuse the right of free speech, those who try to lead us for personal gain or fame, lies not in the elimination of our rights or even putting a stop to people who dupe us, but in our ability to become better listeners. The more effective our listening skills, the more knowledge we possess to help us accurately steer our own course in life.

The effects of poor listening are monumental and can even result in disastrous consequences. The results of effective listening are infinite. Improving your listening skills can only result in positive consequences. Furthermore, the risks involved in becoming a more effective listener are almost nonexistent!

Reasons We Don't Listen,
And Overcoming Barriers to Listening

Reasons We Don't Listen

If listening is so beneficial, so rewarding, virtually risk-free and advantageous in personal and professional life, then why do so few of us use it effectively? There are several answers to this question. Some are reasons; some are excuses. All are important to understand if you wish to pursue the improvement of your listening skills.

We will examine several reasons why we don't listen, what effects result, and ways to overcome nonlistening behaviors. If these behaviors are familiar to you (and we believe they will be), then you have taken the first step toward improving your skills. Being aware of our motivations is an important step to understanding why we do what we do. By having a clear understanding of how and why you fail to listen, you will have begun the process necessary to improve.

The main reason we often fail to listen is because of habits we have formed about listening. Most habits become so ingrained as behaviors that we simply do them without consciously thinking about them. You get up in the morning, stumble into the bathroom and start brushing your teeth. Why? Because you're afraid of tooth decay, gum disease, or that Mom will yell? Probably none of the above. While these may have been factors in originally getting you to brush, the act is now a habit. The same type of response is true about how and when you listen. All of the following reasons for poor listening fall under the general category of habits that have been formed over years of development.

While most of us intellectually know that interpersonal communication requires listeners and speakers to function, most of us tend to forget that factor and concentrate on *talking*. Our desire to speak and present our own opinions becomes a habit. While someone else is talking, we find our thoughts drifting to what we want to say as soon as possible. Consequently, we quit listening or fail to listen altogether. This love of our own voice can be traced to the fact that talking in our society seems to be more advantageous than listening. Think about it. From the time we are born we are encouraged to talk. "Say 'dada, mama'; I wonder what the baby's first words will be? Jessica said 'go out' today. What a good girl! Mommy and Daddy are so proud of her!" Not until much later, if ever, do we consider whether the child is listening. At parties the person talking and joking is considered to be having a good time while the person sitting and listening is labeled a "wallflower." Or take the example of politicians. Who gets elected to office? The person who speaks, or the listener? Obviously, the speaker, and this is just the opposite of what should happen. Our elected officials are supposed to be listening to us. Just with these few examples it's easy to see why it seems more rewarding to talk than to listen.

Another habit that leads to poor listening is the belief that listening is a *passive activity*. We make the assumption that communication is primarily the responsibility of the person speaking. All we have to do as listeners is to sit back and let the words flow in. While there are many faults with this belief, the primary difficulty lies in the fact that the words the speaker uses do not always mean the same thing to the receiver as the sender meant them to. The basic assumption is that if you heard what was said, then you understood the message. This simply isn't true. It is the responsibility of the listener to use feedback to confirm the understanding. To overcome this barrier you must make a decision to listen and give feedback. Check out what you thought you heard. Misunderstandings can quickly be remedied before problems occur.

A third habit that has been labeled the *entertainment syndrome* (23) is another reason we may fail to listen. This refers to the idea that most poor listeners hold the belief that says "I do not have to listen to anything that isn't entertaining, amusing, or interesting." Since a great deal of information and communication fails to fall into this category, the poor listener feels justified in ignoring much of what is said to him. It is true that good speakers will attempt to interest and keep an audience's attention to what they say; but should the speaker fail to achieve this goal, it still does not negate the possible importance of what he has to say. Your boss may not be a lively, entertaining speaker, but tuning him out might cause several problems later. A good listener seeks to *get* the information presented, even if it's not "enjoyable" to do so. Next time you find yourself less than entertained by a speaker, remember that you aren't losing anything by really listening, and you might gain from the interaction.

The fourth habit, that of *assumption and biases*, is one of the most detrimental of all hazards to listening. Assumptions are beliefs that we hold to be true. For instance, you may assume that something is unimportant or doesn't affect you. This assumption may be true or it may not be. They are decisions we make and then continue to make by taking them for granted. *Biases* grow out of our assumptions. They are likes and dislikes, our preferences and prejudices. Several problems can arise when we allow these beliefs to interfere with our listening. Here are some examples that illustrate this fact: We assume that we've heard the information before and cease to listen. We assume the lecture is too difficult to understand, so we tune out.

An example of biases causing listening problems can be seen if we look at a discussion of capital punishment. Let us say that you are biased in favor of capital punishment, i.e., the death penalty. You are supposed to be listening to a speaker who is discussing the opposite viewpoint. Because of your bias you may not even listen to the speaker, or you may misinterpret what is said. You may believe the person said things she didn't, or add messages that were not included. The same applies to the times when we fail to listen to someone due to assumptions we believe about certain people. If we believe that someone is disreputable, we tend not to listen to him because of his personality. Most of us have been guilty at one time or another of just such conduct. If we have already formed some conceptions of what this person is like, we will tend not to listen or distort what he says. Take, for example, the hypothetical Mr. Con. Mr. Con has recently been released from prison after spending seven years incarcerated for armed robbery. You are informed that he will be speaking to your class the next day. Now, due to society's belief that criminals are just that and have no redeeming grace, many people would choose either to skip class that day or come and not listen. But let's suppose that Mr. Con is speaking on ways to burgler-proof your house and car. By choosing not to listen because of the reputation of the speaker you might miss some valuable and useful information. The key is to listen first for information and then apply any assumptions you may possess about the believability or worth of the data.

None of the previous statements is intended to imply that assumptions and biases are inherently wrong. Everyone has them, and they are even desirable at times. The point here is that when these beliefs interfere with our listening, they can cause problems. Perhaps a good deterrent to this type of behavior is to remember the following story. My uncle had a sign on his desk that looked like this: ASS/U/ME. When asked what this meant he would reply, "Every time you assume, you make an ass out of you and me." It has always been a rather graphic reminder to me to listen first and then apply my assumptions *after* getting the whole picture.

Distractions can also cause problems in listening. Distractions or noise is anything that interferes with the communication process. There are basically three categories of distractions that are factors in poor listening behavior.

The first problem is when a physical hearing problem exists. If a person has a permanent or even temporary hearing loss, he cannot listen as well as one with normal hearing. When was the last time you had your hearing checked? A large percentage of the American population has minor hearing losses that they are unaware of. Even minor problems that may be caused from a cold or swimmer's ear can affect our listening. If you have a hearing problem, don't be afraid or embarrassed to inform the person speaking of it. This way he can help you listen to what he has to say. If one ear is better than the other, sit with your good ear turned towards the source. This can be done inconspicuously. Hearing problems can be overcome and your listening will dramatically improve.

The second is external noise. These are distractions ourside our ears like the TV, loud machinery, children crying or even a smoky room. They make it difficult to pay attention to what is being said and can even make it difficult to hear, let alone listen. Take the phone off the hook; turn off the radio; tell the kids to play outside. A student described a situation that is probably pretty common to many of us. She got home at about 2:30 in the afternoon. Her son arrived about 3:00. He had lots to tell his mom about his day's activities and plans. She would be cleaning, fixing supper, or answering the phone. She wanted to listen, but there was so much to do! After awhile she discovered her son would come home and go to his room without so much as a "Hi, Mom. I'm home." This bothered her. She loved her son and wanted to share his highs and lows with him, so she corrected the situation. As soon as the young man arrived home, the TV was turned off and the phone was taken off the hook for half an hour. They sat down for that half hour or longer and she listened to him. It worked the other way as well: He listened to her, and their relationship grew and improved. She hadn't lost a half hour cooking and cleaning; she had gained a better understanding and a life-time relationship with an important person in her life. There were fewer fights, more obedience, helping, and general harmony in their lives. She had also taught her son a valuable listening tool to use in his life.

The last category is that of internal noises or preoccupation. Essentially, this is the "noise" you hear between your ears. It is daydreaming about the weekend, or thinking about your math test during your English class. When we are preoccupied with our own thoughts, we find it difficult to listen to others. Whatever you are preoccupied with when you are supposed to be listening can always be returned to, but chances are that the person speaking will not be repeating his message. Simple, isn't it? And yet it is a very effective way to learn to listen. Obviously the point is to concentrate on the message being sent. By tuning in to the message you only postpone what was on your mind. It is easily retrieved. Nothing is lost, and you have gained new information from the message you listened to.

The sixth cause of nonlistening is *fear of the material* being presented. If we believe that what is being said is above our level of understanding, we may decide it would be a waste of time to listen. Other situations that may lead to the same type of avoidance are found when we have already established our stand on an issue or behavior and are fearful of listening and possibly being persuaded to change. If you smoke cigarettes, you may not listen to a speaker who is anti-smoking. If you listen, you will be subjected to all the arguments against such a habit and will either have to change, or live with the fact that you are purposefully damaging your health. Most of us would rather avoid (i.e., not listen to) the situation altogether. But, we can listen to other viewpoints without changing our own (see Perception Chapter). On the contrary, by listening we enhance our own perspectives without changing our views.

Another reason we don't listen is due to *message overload*. As we stated in the first part of this chapter, over half of our waking hours are spent in activities which require us to listen. Our friends, family, co-workers and teachers talk to us. We listen to the radio and TV. It isn't possible to be attentive at all times with so much verbiage hitting us from all sides. The important thing to remember here is that even though we may be tired of listening, if it's important, we must strive to pay attention. Sometimes it is useful, but not always possible, to give ourselves a few minutes of total quiet before a period when we know we will be required to listen. Driving to work or school without the radio on or without talking to someone may help you to prepare for the onslaught of all the messages you will be expected to receive.

A mental process known as the *speaking/thinking rate* is another culprit that harms listening. People are capable of understanding speech 4 to 5 times faster than the average person actually speaks. Because of this discrepancy we have a lot of extra time mentally while someone is speaking. The tendency is to use this "spacetime" to let our minds wander, become preoccupied with our own thoughts and fail to pay attention to the speaker. A question that is often asked when this problem is discussed in class is this: "If I can understand someone 4 to 5 times faster than people usually speak, then why can't I understand someone when they speak faster than normal?" The answer to this question refers to the section we have discussed on assumptions and biases. Since we are used to hearing people talk at a certain rate, any faster delivery is perceived as too fast. We assume we won't understand, so we quit listening. Keep on the same track as the speaker. Ask a question, either out loud or to yourself. Use the extra time to enhance the message by application to your own experience.

The last reason we will discuss as a reason we don't listen is perhaps the most important. *We are not trained to listen.* Did you ever take a class devoted to teaching you how to listen? Did your parents ever sit you down and say, "O.K., Ashley, this is what you do to listen"? Probably not. There are the infrequent classes on critical listening taught to music majors, or a chapter on active listening given to speech or psychology majors; but even these courses don't actually *teach* the student day-to-day skills needed to listen. Most of us assume that if we can hear, we listen; or because we've been listening for years, we don't have to study it. The fact is that while everyone engages in listening, few of us do it well.

Listening is a skill, just like any other skill, and it can be learned. It is not easy to listen, but with dedication, time and some useful practical steps you can improve your listening skills and reap the benefits. Keeping the reasons we don't listen in mind and becoming more aware of times we fall into nonlistening behaviors will start you towards improving your listening capabilities.

Nonlistening Styles*

Ron Adler and Neil Towne have identified seven nonlistening styles. These are categories that describe people who fail to listen. While there is a danger in labeling and grouping that can lead to faulty assumptions, we include them because they are common factors that disturb the listening process. As you read about these behaviors, try and remember when you may have been guilty of using them.

Pseudolistening is pretending to listen. It is an imitation of the real thing. This is a frequent behavior that most of us use. Smiling, nodding and saying "yes" to a speaker when you have no idea what he said, is a form of pseudo-listening.

Stagehogging is not listening because you don't allow anyone else to say anything. The person who stagehogs isn't interested in others' ideas; she is too enamoured of her own voice and opinions.

Selective listening refers to the times when we ignore most of what is said. We "tune-in" or listen only when the conversation is about the subject we are interested in.

Insulated listening is the process of "tuning out" a conversation when the subject is not to our liking. We may listen to what is being said, but as soon as the topic turns to diet, cleaning our room or politics, we quit listening.

Defensive listening occurs when we take what is said as a personal attack, even though it was meant as an innocent remark. An example of this behavior is as follows: Someone says, "Gee, you look nice today!" Your reply is, "I suppose you mean I don't usually look good!" You've used defensive listening: taking a sincere compliment as a personal attack.

Ambushing is listening to get information to use against the speaker. It is actually a listening behavior, but because of its purpose it falls into these categories. The ambusher listens carefully to what you say for the purpose of collecting ammunition to use to attack you.

DENNIS THE MENACE

"OH-OH! HERE COMES MARGARET LOOKING FOR A GOOD LISTENER!"

Dennis The Menace® used by permission of Hank Ketcham and © by News American Syndicate.

Insensitive listening is taking the words that are said literally and not applying any of the nonverbals or paralinguistics to the message. An insensitive listener might hear someone say "Oh, you're wonderful, alright!" and believe that's what the speaker meant and would not have understood or perceived the intended sarcasm.

If you find yourself using one or a combination of the nonlistening styles often, you can probably see that you need to decrease their use to become a better listener. Even if you believe you use them infrequently, you can still see that whenever they are used, they keep you from fully listening.

Knowing the importance of improving listening skills, the factors that influence us to not listen, and ways we fail to listen brings us to the next step: You are now more fully aware of the complications in listening and can begin to actually improve your listening skills.

There is no clear cut program that upon completion will assure you improved listening skills. There are, however, numerous ways in which you personally can better these skills. Being aware of the problems of poor listening and knowing the benefits of effective listening may have led you to believe you want to improve your skills. With dedication you can make a difference. The following steps, if practiced diligently, can make a big difference in how you listen.

A Practical Approach to Listening Improvement*

There are three basic steps to becoming a more effective listener. They are recognition, refusal, and replacement. We will examine each step separately.

Recognition is the first necessary process in becoming a better listener. Recognition refers to becoming aware of present habits. Before any change can take place, you must be aware of the current behavior. Just as you must be aware of the problems in any context before you can fix them, so it is with improving your listening skills.

An effective way of monitoring your poor habits is to make a list of them. This can be accomplished by keeping a nonlistening diary for 3-5 days.

Nonlistening Diary Exercise

1. For 3-5 days keep track of your nonlistening behaviors; i.e., the times you failed to listen to what was said.

2. Concisely describe the situation: who was speaking, what was said, etc.?

3. Label the nonlistening style you used for each situation. (Refer to pp. 68-69 of this section for the seven nonlistening styles.)

4. State the reason you didn't listen. (Refer to pp. 63-68 for reasons we don't listen.)

5. After completion of the time period, review and summarize what you have learned about your personal nonlistening behavior.

Once you have recognized these problems, you can begin to change them. The previous exercise should have helped you identify the people, situations and topics that trigger your nonlistening behaviors. Chances are these behaviors have become habits. True, it will be difficult to first, be aware of, and second, adjust the behavior, but it can be done.

*From *Listening: A Practical Approach* by James J. Floyd. Copyright © 1985 by Scott, Forsman and Company. Reprinted by permission.

Monitor your listening behavior in order to catch yourself when you begin to tune out. Having done the nonlistening diary, you will be more aware of the times when you are likely not to listen. When you find yourself participating in a poor listening habit, you must immediately give yourself a "mental slap" and tune back in. This will not be easy. Due to the nature of habits, we tend to engage in them without much conscious thought. It will take conscious effort to change habits that have developed over a lifetime, but don't give up. Remember that the changes and benefits will come with dedication and time.

The second step is *refusal*. This means that once you have recognized your listening problems, you must dedicate yourself to stopping those habits. This is easier said than done. Perhaps an analogy will help you understand.

Pretend you are on a diet. You know that losing weight is beneficial to your health and appearance. You know the symptoms that send you to the refrigerator, but that alone doesn't stop you from munching. Most of us have a tendency to rationalize that one cupcake won't make a difference. Still we fail to lose weight and achieve our goal. It isn't until we stop ourselves from reaching for that snack that we really have achieved the step of *refusal*. Unfortunately, this battle must be fought over and over again because old habits are hard to break. It is the automatic response we must control.

The same is true when we try to change our listening habits. Aunt Martha is talking about her car accident for the four-hundredth time. We tune out: a habit, a conditioned response. Change occurs only when we recognize the response and refuse to take part in that behavior.

The final step is that of *replacement*. Replacement is the process that substitutes positive listening habits for old, ineffectual ones. It is a natural step that follows refusal. As you keep yourself from practicing old habits, you can replace them with desirable listening behaviors. As you repeatedly change your behavior, you will be developing new skills and habits conducive to better listening.

Active Listening

Once you have mastered day-to-day listening skills, you may find it useful to learn a listening technique called *active listening*. This method was developed by Thomas Gorden in his "effectiveness" seminars and workshops. It is a specific set of skills used when someone comes to you with a problem. Before we begin learning how to use this method, we will look at the usual ways people respond to those who come to them with problems.

Typical Ways of Responding

Let's pretend your best friend is having difficulties in dealing with her parents' attitude about her choice of majors in college. You're having lunch together and she says this:

> I really don't know what to do. My folks insist that I major in nursing, but I really want to be in theatre. That's what I really love and get excited about. They say drama is ok for fun but for "real life" I've got to be a nurse.

What would you say? Take time to write down your response before reading any farther. Now, see if your response to your friend fits into one or more of the following categories.

Advertising — This is the style the majority of people use most often. It is responding by giving solutions to the problem such as this: "What I would do is . . ." "Have you ever tried . . ." "Talk to them . . ." and on and on with helpful suggestions and advice. What's wrong with this? After all, they came to you for a solution, didn't they? Maybe not. Chances are that while your friend has a problem and would certainly like a solution to the dilemma, they aren't really asking you to solve it. The majority of the time when people voice their problems, they simply want to share them with someone. Sharing a problem can be cathartic, but the solution must come from the person with the problem. All the advice in the world won't solve anything unless the person in the situation views it as his solution. In addition, we can never be sure the advice we give is 100% right, which can cause further problems. Did you ever advise someone to do something and then have it backfire? You tell a friend to try it; they do; and then come back to you angry and defensive because it made matters worse. You now have a new problem that didn't exist before. Clearly advising isn't the best way to handle the situation. However, if you believe you must respond with advice, try to follow these rules:

1. Make sure the person is specifically asking for your opinion.
2. Offer your best possible solution, being extremely careful to be as correct as you can.
3. Give the advice as a suggestion, not an absolute remedy.
4. Make sure they won't blame you if the suggestion doesn't work.

Judging — When we judge, we evaluate what is said. We respond positively or negatively to what is said or done. This includes such phrases as these: "That's exactly what you should do . . ." "That's stupid . . ." "You'll never get anywhere doing that!" With these responses we are actually setting ourselves in a superior position to the person with the problem. These types of answers are extremely defense producing. Even a favorable response can lead to defensive behavior which is counterproductive to the solution of problems. Someone may practically beg you to tell him your opinion and when he receives it, react very hostilely. In addition, while your friend may value your opinion, your evaluation won't really help solve the problem. Should you feel it is absolutely necessary to respond judgmentally, try to follow these rules:

1. Make sure you have been requested to pass on an opinion.
2. Try to make the evaluation as positive and constructive as possible.
3. Use "I language" not "you language" in your evaluation. Respond with statements that start like, "What *I* think..." In *my* opinion...," etc., not *"You're* right." *"You're* making the wrong decision."* etc.

Analyzing — This type of response involves interpretations of the message sent. Such words as, "What your real problem is..." "She thinks maybe..." "You probably mean...," are all analyses of the problem. While it is necessary to interpret all communication to a certain extent, this type of answer has the same problems as other typical ways of responding. We cannot be sure our interpretation is correct and it can be taken defensively by the person with the problem. However, since interpretation and analysis can be useful aids in solving problems, here are some rules to follow should you find it necessary to do so:

1. Make sure the speaker is requesting your opinion.
2. Offer it as your opinion, not a concrete, absolute fact.
3. Give the reasons for your analysis.
4. Truly want to help the person solve the problem.

Questioning — When we use questions to try to help solve others' problems, we may or may not be helping that person with his problems. Questions can be helpful if they cause the person with the problem to think in the direction he needs to concentrate on to reach a solution; however, all too often the questions we use fall into one of two categories that can lead away from solutions and cause defensiveness. After all, we are really just guessing and could send our friend off on a long, drawn-our explanation that only wastes time. Another type of question that is not helpful is the leading question that teachers and parents seem to be so good at. You know the type — those questions that are really disguised solutions, analyses, or judgments: questions like, "You don't really mean that, do you?" "Did you ever consider that the real problem might be . . ." Questions that try to disguise their real intent seldom help solve problems and often actually lead to more problems due to the defensiveness they tend to produce.

Should you believe that questions would be useful to help solve the problem, try and follow the following suggestions:

1. Don't use leading questions that are really attempts to get the person to respond as you believe they should.
2. Concentrate your questions in the area of the problem. In this way, you can help him clarify the problem without introducing your opinion or causing defensive behavior.
3. Ask open-ended questions that require more than a "yes" or "no" answer.

Supporting — This type of response is the "pat on the back" or the "shoulder to cry on" either literally or figuratively. When someone comes to us with a problem we may try to assure her that all will be well, things will work themselves out, "the sky is always darkest before the dawn," or that she is loved and cared about. Now, on the surface this seems like a perfect response to someone in need. Let's face it, we all need to know that whatever we are facing isn't the end of the world, and we will survive "with a little help from our friends." On the other hand, it doesn't really help solve the problem and it can even cause problems. Simply saying that "all will be well" doesn't make it happen. In most cases when a problem exists, action, not sympathy, is needed. If one is told by others that "it's ok" or "it will fix itself," that person may be inclined to sit back and wait for divine intervention.

While we all need the support and love of our friends and family, there are certain precautions you should take when you are trying to be supportive.

1. Assure the person with the problem that you care about him and that you will gladly listen.
2. Make sure your responses do not infer that the problem will take care of itself.
3. When being supportive, let the other person know that you can't solve his problem and that some sort of action will probably be necessary on his part if a solution is to be found. (Be careful not to suggest what the action should be or you may cause defensiveness.)

Now back to that response you gave the friend with the parental problem of what her major should be. Did your response fall into one or more of these categories? Let's take a look at a better way of responding when people come to us with a problem and we want to help *them* find a solution to their problem.

Active Listening: What is it?

As stated at the beginning of this section, active listening is a technique that can be used when someone comes to you with a problem and you wish to help them solve it. It is usually less defense producing than the typical ways of responding and allows the problem to remain with the person who is involved, not taking it on your shoulders. While you can certainly help someone with his/her problem, the solution must come from the source if it is to be effective.

To use active listening you will simply rephrase what the speaker says, feeding back to them what you heard them say. To do this you must not only concentrate on the verbal message, but also take into consideration the nonverbal elements of the message as well. The whole idea of active listening is to keep the person with the problem talking, so that she can clarify the problem and reach some solution to it. Sometimes it will be necessary to not only mirror her response back, but also hone in on the emotional response as well. Let's look at your friend's statement about her major again.

> I really don't know what to do. My folks insist that I major in nursing, but I really want to be in theatre. That's what I really love and get excited about. They say drama is ok for fun, but for "real life" I've got to be a nurse.

When you paraphrase your friend's words, be careful not to "parrot" them back to her; i.e., don't say them back to her word for word, but put the ideas in your words as you understand them and notice how she says what she says, not only what she says. Does she stress any words? Is she shouting, quiet, or crying? What does her body language imply? Put all these clues together and then respond. Be careful not to imply any judgment or use the other typical ways of responding.

Therefore, an active listening response to your friend might be this: "You and your parents can't agree on what you should major in and you're angry (or nervous, confused, etc.) about their interference." This type of response will let your friend check out what she said and clarify it or continue to discuss it.

When To Use Active Listening

1. Use active listening only when there appears to be a problem that exists. Do not use active listening when someone is clearly asking for information. For example, if someone comes to you and asks, "What time

is it?'', it would be inappropriate to respond with, ''I see that you are concerned about the time.'' On the same note, however, a problem can be worded as if it were asking for information. If someone says, ''What should I do about my poor math grades?'' you should respond with an active listening response because this obviously is a problem that the person needs to solve for himself. Another clue to a problem is if he asks for specific information and you respond, but he keeps asking the same question over and over again. Pretend that you and your spouse traditionally go out for dinner or a movie on Friday night. He comes to you and says, ''Do you want to go out tonight?'' You say, ''Yes.'' He responds with, ''Are you sure you want to go out?'' Chances are there is an underlying problem. Maybe he wants to do something else, or there really isn't enough money this week for the movie. If someone asks an informational question and you respond with an answer, but get asked the same question again, you might want to switch to an active listening response.

2. Use active listening when you have time to give that person your undivided attention. Listening takes time, particularly active listening. There is no way to know exactly how long it might take you to help this person solve his problem. It might take five minutes, or it could take hours. Therefore, before engaging in active listening be sure you won't have to rush off to another appointment or be interrupted by the kids or the telephone. If you would like to help this person, but don't have the time immediately available, it is better to set up an appointment to meet later than to start and be rushed or interrupted.

3. Use active listening when you genuinely are concerned about that person and want to help him. Probably all of us would like to be altruistic and help everyone we come in contact with. Let's be honest. That isn't possible. We all have demands on our time and energies and helping everyone isn't mentally, physically, or emotionally possible. We must set priorities or in the long run we may harm ourselves, those who must depend on us, and the person with the problem. It is not only much kinder, but also practical to nicely inform someone that you really don't believe you can help them, than to lead them on and either be preoccupied by what you aren't accomplishing, or become resentful of the interference they are causing in your life. In the long run a simple, ''I can't help you with that,'' is a better way to handle the situation.

4. Use active listening when you can focus on the speaker and withhold your personal judgments and comments. Remember that active listening focuses on the person with the problem. You need to keep them talking and withhold your ''two cent's worth.'' When you actively listen, you must not try to influence the other person or tell him what he should do, even when

you are sure he is headed in the wrong direction! This is very difficult, particularly since you care about that person (or you wouldn't be actively listening to begin with) and you don't want to see him hurt. Just remember that he is the one with the problem and only he can solve it. The solutions that work are always the ones the person with the problem believes will work. That solution may be the same one you would have given him hours ago, but until he believes it and finds it for himself, it won't be his solution.

When the previous rules are used, you will find that active listening has advantages over those typical ways that most people use when someone comes to them with a problem. It is certainly less defense producing and usually results in a better, more effective solution to the matter at hand. Active listening is not always easy to use and certainly should not be used at all times, but when used correctly and practiced, it becomes easier and more effective. Try starting with smaller problems others try to involve you in. Then, with a couple of successful interactions under your belt, you can help others you care about solve their own problems.

Conclusion

Listening is an important survival skill. It involves much more than simply hearing what is said. If you increase your level of listening, you will find that your life will improve in numerous ways. It won't be easy to replace old habits, but it will be worth it.

Bibliography

Bonville, Thomas. *How to Listen, How to be Heard.* Chicago: Nelson-Hall, 1978.
DeVita, Joseph A. *The Interpersonal Communication Book.* New York: Harper & Row Publishers, 1983.
Floyd, James. *Listening: A Practical Approach.* Glenview, IL: Scott, Forsman and Company, 1985.
Keefe, Wm. F. *Listen, Management! Creative Listening for Better Managing.* New York: McGraw-Hill, 1971.
Lane, Margaret. "Are You Really Listening?" *Reader's Digest,* November, 1980, 183-184.
Wolff, Florence I., Nadine D. Marsnik, William S. Tacey, Ralph G. Nichols. *Perceptive Listening.* New York: Holt, Rinehart and Winston, 1983.

5

Perception

I. Two general categories that regulate perception.
    A. Physiological factors.
        1. Taste.
        2. Odor.
        3. Sight.
        4. Hearing.
        5. Temperature.
        6. Height and weight.
        7. Fatigue.
        8. Hunger.
        9. Health.
    B. Cultural Expectations.
        1. Origin.
        2. Subcultures.
        3. Occupational roles.
        4. Sex roles.

II. Two principles of perception.
    A. The perceived is a combination of itself and the perceiver.
    B. Perception is selective.

III. Dealing with perceptual differences.
    A. Listen carefully.
    B. Be creative.
    C. Empathize with your partner.
    D. Agree to disagree.

Introduction

"What you see is what you get!"

Several years ago, comedian Flip Wilson (dressed as a woman) made this statement popular. It was used by people to mean that what you saw was what you got, no more, no less, nothing hidden or left out. This statement, simple and straightforward, couldn't be more deceptive. Take a look at the following diagram and see why. *How many squares do you count?*

How many did you count—24, 28, 30? Fewer? More? The answer is 40. They're there as individual and combined figures. Is what you saw what you got? The diagram is simple, straightforward, nothing hidden, nothing left out and yet chances are you didn't arrive at 40 squares in the diagram. Furthermore, there were probably several *different* answers given by your classmates. You all saw the same diagram, or did you? Does the person who saw 24 squares only see that many, therefore only getting a total of 24? What about the person who saw 35? Where did he get 11 more squares? Is his diagram different from yours? The answer lies not in the diagram (what you see), but rather in how you perceived that diagram (what you got).

Perception, the act of categorizing and interpreting sense data, causes communication difficulties. Since no two people have exactly the same environments, no two people share exactly the same perception. On one hand, if we could somehow manage to have everyone perceive things the same way, come to the same conclusions, we would probably eliminate 99 percent of all communication breakdowns. On the other hand, such total agreement would probably make for a boring world. Obviously, this total sharing of perceptions isn't possible, practical or even desirable. So why study perception at all? If you can't "fix" it, what's the use? The reason we need to study this phenomenon is to reduce the complications, the unnecessary arguments, hurt feelings and general misunderstandings that differences in perception often lead to. We may not be able to eliminate all communication breakdowns, but through understanding and empathy, we can learn to treat differences in opinion for what they are—everyone's right to his or her perception.

Our perceptions are based upon and affected by two general categories: physiological reactions and cultural expectations.

Physiological Effects on Perception

Many of the disagreements that occur in our lives are results of physical perceptions. In other words, many of the problems in agreement are direct results of how we feel physically or how our body is reacting. These physiological effects are results that occur over which we have little to no control. No amount of reason or argument will change the perception.

While there are many related physiological responses, let's take a look at nine common ones to explain the previous statements.

Taste—What we commonly refer to as taste, determining the flavor of something, is actually a chemical reaction of body secretions and the compounds in the food and drink in our mouths. This is a normal biological function that happens automatically and we have no control over it. Several people may taste the same food with varying results. One person may say it is salty, one may describe it as sweet and yet another may label it as bland, having little or no flavor at all. Why the difference in perception? Each person has a different body chemistry that reacts with the food causing these diverse opinions. No matter how much discussion takes place, an agreement in perception will never be reached. It is futile and a waste of time to argue this type of perception.

Think about the flavor of something that you liked or didn't like when you were a child and now have a different opinion of. Was the taste of liver awful and bitter? What about the Indian spice, curry? Was it too "hot" and spicy? Consider the taste of various alcoholic beverages. Most children do not like the taste of alcohol, but perceptions may change as they grow older. What's the difference? Why the change in perception? Probably a natural change in your body chemistry; you didn't necessarily learn to like it, you physically changed causing a shift in perception.

Odor—The smell of something is another physical reaction caused by our individual body makeup. While you may agree upon what smells good or bad in some instances, chances are you have had disagreements about a particular odor as well. Studies have found that our age and sex play an important part in our perception of various smells. Men and children tend to like the smell of sweetness and earthy musk smells more than women do. Children not only tolerate, but like many odors that adults find unpleasant. It is obvious from these studies that perception based on smells is directly related to physical reactions. Try the following exercise and then compare your response to the exercise with your classmates.

Rank the following five smells in the order of your preference. Number 1 would be the smell you like the most from the list and number 5 would be what you like the least.

> Cooked onions
>
> Gasoline
>
> The interior of a new car
>
> Burning leaves
>
> Earth after a rain

After comparing your list with others in the class you probably discovered that there were a variety of different rankings. Since odors are perceived through a physical means, you can see that there is no right or wrong response, just differing ones. Again it is practically useless to argue over these differences because without changing the other person's body chemistry, you probably will not change their opinion.

Sight—Since we obviously see by using our eyes, it isn't difficult to understand why sight is involved in the physical perception process. We are aware that some people can see better than others. After all, people often have to wear corrective eye lenses to bring their vision up to the norm. However, knowing this and being able to understand when vision causes perception problems is far more complex than it would appear. Very often we misunderstand someone or get into a defensive shouting match because we fail to realize that the problem is really a physical one. The following example proves this very point.

When I was in college, a girlfriend and I used to go on long car trips. We very often would drive all night and by dawn would be in territory that neither one of us was familiar with. This necessitated the use of a map and navigator while the other person drove. My friend would only drive during daylight hours, on a fairly straight road, in dry weather conditions. Obviously this meant that most of the driving was done by me, while she navigated. The problem was that we would often have passed an exit before she told me we should take it. One day, when it had been raining — we were in the mountains of Virginia and had been driving through the night — she failed to tell me about an exit that caused a major change in plans. I pulled off the road and said, "Look, I've been driving all night because you won't. It's raining and you won't drive. The roads are switch-backs, so you won't drive. Now we're 50 miles in the middle of nowhere and you can't even read a simple road map. What's wrong with you!" She looked at me as if she would like to get out and walk back to Illinois and said, "I can't see the map!" Suddenly I realized that I had almost picked a fight over a problem that wasn't of her making. We both wore contact lenses so I assumed that we both had normal vision. What I didn't understand until that moment was that her sight was so much poorer than mine that even with corrections she saw much less than I. That also explained why she would only drive under ideal circumstances. She could barely see to drive when it was daylight and not wet, and the twists in the highways frightened her because she didn't see them until she was right on top of them. I learned a valuable lesson that day. I had almost lost a good friend because I didn't understand why she perceived things the way she did based on the sense of sight.

Hearing — This refers to the physical function of your ears. Hearing is a reverberation of sound waves on the eardrum. It is probably safe to assume that most of you have had a difference of opinion with someone that was caused by this physical occurrence. Usually the scene goes something like this: You are listening to music on the stereo or radio or perhaps watching TV. You are comfortable with the volume of the sound but suddenly a voice yells out, "Turn that down, it's too loud!" Sound familiar? This is a common perceptual problem. You don't think the music is too loud or you would have decreased the volume yourself. Obviously, human beings have different levels of hearing. Other problems that are caused by lack of hearing are often responsible for creating defensive behavior. If you say something to someone and they don't respond, you feel ignored. You believe that they are slighting you on purpose. If you know that hearing can cause perception problems, then you are more willing to investigate the cause. A large percentage of the time we will find that we weren't being ignored; the other person simply had not heard what we said.

Temperature— What's hot and what's cold seems like a straightforward factual conclusion. Nothing could be further from the truth. Ninety degrees Fahrenheit is factual; "that's hot" is a perceptual opinion based on physiological data. Our perception of temperature is based on a number of physical reactions: our metabolic rate, how much we perspire, the thickness of our skin, etc. These vary from person to person and are what we base our interpretations on. A classic example that many people have shared illustrates this perception at work: It's summer and time to go swimming for the first time. You and a group of friends head for the beach, pool or pond and get ready for that all-important dip. An adventurer among you dives into the water. You ask, "How's the water?" Your friend responds, "Great!" You take the plunge and emerge from the water shivering and turning blue. What was fine for your friend was not comfortable for you. Chances are, your friend wasn't trying to be mean, but honestly felt the water temperature was comfortable for swimming. The difference is purely a physical response and no amount of cajoling will convince you to return to the water. Remember that temperature is a physical perception and the next time someone tells you to turn down the heat, he isn't attacking you, but merely expressing his perception.

Height and Weight— These physical characteristics are often talked about, yet rarely do we think that they are causes of physical perception disagreements. It is perhaps easiest to understand if you picture an average person whose weight and height fall into the normal ranges and a person who is of greater or lesser weight or height than the norm. With this picture in your mind you can understand that a comfortable chair to the person 5 feet 6 inches, weighing about 145 pounds, is *not* a comfortable chair to someone who is 6 feet 4 inches tall and weighs close to 300 pounds. Perhaps an even more common occurrence is the perception of a child's physical characteristics compared to those of an adult. Children literally see things differently and experience different sensations due to their diminutive size. The simple act of turning on a water faucet becomes a monumental task for the short child who must overcome the height problem before turning on the faucet. These physical differences can often lead to misunderstandings that cause communication breakdowns.

Point of view — Height and Weight

Fatigue—When we are tired, we perceive things differently than when we are alert and full of energy. If we lack energy due to lack of sleep or because of over-exertion, we will tend to perceive simple tasks as too strenuous, whereas under normal circumstances we would easily be able to accomplish them. All too often when someone replies that he is too tired to do something, we tend to think that he is just giving an excuse or being lazy, yet this may not be the case. Most people tend to label themselves "day" or "night" people. By doing this they are referring to that time of day when they feel most alert and are most likely to enjoy and accomplish more. This is the physical sensation of energy at work. If, at 6:00 a.m., you wake up to the alarm and still feel groggy and unrested, you will perceive things differently from the person who jumps out of bed rested and full of energy. It should be remembered that since fatigue is a physical characteristic, no amount of argument will change a person's perception. Only rest will alleviate the problem, allowing the person to change her perception.

Hunger—When we are physically hungry and our body needs nourishment, we will perceive things on a different scale than when we are satisfied after eating. Food and water are two of man's basic needs and must be satisfied before he can move on to the satisfaction of other desires. Therefore, if we are hungry, we will concentrate on our physical need before anything else. Mothers and fathers know that when an infant is hungry, the only way to quiet the child is to feed him. No amount of bouncing or talking will comfort him. He needs to eat and he needs to eat now! Adults aren't much different than children when it comes to fulfilling the desire to eat. While we adults may be able to sustain the need to eat for a longer period of time, it will still be of primary concern to us. Think about the last time you missed a couple of meals in a row or were on a low calorie diet. You didn't necessarily fulfill the hunger when you wanted to, but chances are good that eating was on your mind. Because food is a primary concern of human beings, when this need is not met, we will have more disagreements because our basic need will be more important than anything else that is occurring. This is important to know if you wish to cut down on problems that arise due to hunger. If you have a problem that needs discussion and the other person is hungry, it is best to feed him first. Did you ever notice that if dinner is late, tempers tend to flare, or that children tend to get into arguments and fights while you are trying to put the finishing touches on dinner? The reason is due to the physical sensation of hunger that causes perception problems. A good rule of thumb to follow is: If you discover a difference in opinion and either of the involved parties is hungry, suggest dinner. It just might make a difference.

Health—If you are physically ill, you have a headache, the flu or a cold, you will perceive things in a more negative light than if you were feeling well. Speaking purely physically, our health is a major factor in our perceptual process. I'm sure you have observed that people who aren't feeling well tend to be crabby and short-tempered. They don't see things the way they did yesterday or even an hour earlier, before the headache hit. Since our health and well-being are of primary importance to us, we find it difficult to concentrate on anything other than how miserable we are feeling when we are suffering from some malady. Even though we may be capable of functioning, as opposed to being sick enough to be in bed, our perceptual processes will be severely undermined. We think less clearly, have a shorter attention span, and tend to resent trying to accomplish anything other than feeling better. We are best advised to refrain from engaging in any important discussions or decisions that could involve major differences of opinion, until all parties involved are feeling well.

By realizing that all these factors play an important role in our perceptual processes, we will more easily be able to spot possible problems. In addition, when we do run into differences of opinions, we can quickly analyze the factors involved and try to determine if any of the factors leading to these perceptions are caused by physiological causes. If we discover this to be the case, we have two options open to us. We can try to eliminate the problem if possible by trying to correct it; such as adjusting a volume, or suggesting lunch if the person is hungry, before trying to come to an agreement; or we can accept the fact that it is a physical perception difference and that it's probably beyond the control of the individual and can't be changed. Under the second view, we will save a lot of time and energy that would be wasted trying to get others to perceive things our way when they are unable to, due to differing body chemistries, sizes, etc.

The other category that affects our perceptions is cultural expectations. Unlike physiological effects, these perceptions are based on social and cultural influences and can be altered by the people involved.

Effects of Cultural Expectations on Perception

The culture, society, or country we are raised in affects the way we perceive things. Unlike physiological effects that are inherent in our body makeup, these cultural factors are learned from an early age. While these are learned phenomenon, we cannot necessarily imply that we have logically examined these effects and can justify our perceptions by factual reasoning. As a matter of fact, the simple acceptance of many of these expectations leads to arguments when people from different backgrounds, social norms, or sexes discover their differing perceptions.

Origin— The country that we live in has certain rules and regulations that govern how we function in that society. Some of these are in the form of actual laws, but a far geater number are accepted as social norms and aren't in print. As an American who grew up in the United States you accept certain behaviors as appropriate and others as inappropriate. While eating in a fancy restaurant, you would never use your fingers to eat your mashed potatoes. This is a social norm. It isn't written at the top of the menu or posted above the cash register, nor is it legally a law that is punishable by a fine or imprisonment; still we don't do it. It is perceived as impolite or not mannerly to do so. That's what social norms are, those unwritten laws that most of us live by. Social norms, however, are not the same throughout the world. They differ from country to country and in fact, from region to region within countries. In the United States, physical contact with another person we don't know well is usually limited to a handshake or a nod of the head that eliminates any need for physical contact. A hug, kiss or pinch would be deemed socially unacceptable in the U.S. This is not the case in Italy. Upon an introduction in that country (or even without an introduction in some cases), you can expect a hug, a kiss, or some other form of physical demonstration that Americans believe to be an intrusion on their personal space. This is a cultural perception. Many a visitor to our country has been embarrassed by reacting the way they would in their country only to find that such behavior is inappropriate in our country. We have probably all heard stories and reports about the behavior of Americans in other countries. We are labeled rude, unthinking or the proverbial "Ugly American." In most cases this is caused by a cultural perception. We Americans are doing what we would find acceptable in our country and it is interpreted differently in the country we are in.

Even when we aren't traveling, we can run into differences of perception caused by origin differences. Our country is known as the "melting pot," which means that we assimilate many cultures and people of various nations into our society. The southwest has large groups of Hispanic people and many metropolitan areas have large groups of Asian, Italian, Polish, or other cultural backgrounds. These groups tend to live together in one area or region and continue to speak their native language and preserve customs from their land of origin. Because of this, even second and third generations who were born in the United States may follow the original social norms and customs that are traditional in their families. When we run into problems that are based on cultural perceptions due to the country of origin, we must understand why the differences are there. Only then can we attempt to come to some type of understanding.

Subcultures — Subcultures are groups of people united by some common denominator. They are smaller in number than the greater society, but still may number large percentages of a nation. Subcultures include people who have the same religious beliefs, are of the same racial group, live in one particular region of a country, and many other common groups of people. The same type of perception occurs between the greater society and its subcultures that exist between two different cultures or countries. The perceptual problems that arise when two subcultures clash can cause major problems in a society. Any time people perceive others to be *different* from themselves there is potential for broad-ranging communication breakdowns that often lead to severe disturbances. The armed and warring factions in Ireland are just such a case. While Ireland is one country, it has divided itself into two factions, the Catholics and the Protestants. These two religious subcultures have been responsible for bombings, deaths, riots and other massive problems within this one small country. The problems have snowballed into vast political, social and personal complications, but the root of all these lie in the differences of perception caused by the religious subcultural differences.

America is not without her subcultural problems either. You are all probably familiar with jokes that make fun of a certain subculture's intelligence or basic knowledge. These same jokes are common across the U.S., but the group often changes depending upon the subcultures that are prevalent in the area of the country where the joke is being told. On the surface, these attempts at humor may seem innocent and fun, but they carry with them the potential for real danger. When we make fun of a subculture, we are in essence showing our prejudice against that group of people. Prejudice is a major perceptual problem. When we are prejudiced against any group (subculture), we are really displaying our ignorance of that group's standards. At other times we use our limited perception of one or a small number within a subculture and randomly apply it to the entirety. These perceptual problems can and have led our country to massive outbreaks of violence and disharmony. Again, perceptual differences have caused communication breakdowns that lead us away from understanding and agreement.

Since subcultural perceptions are learned, not inherent biologically, they may seem "easier to fix." Unfortunately, this isn't true. Beliefs that people hold strongly, even if they have little to back them up, are often just as deeply ingrained as the physiological functions that affect perception. As a matter of fact those subcultural perceptions based strictly on faith are almost as difficult, if not impossible, to change as it would be to try to convince someone that what they perceive to be cool is really warm.

Occupational Roles— Americans are divided into classes by what appears to be economical standards. We talk about the upper, middle and lower classes which at first glance seems to refer to income levels. The real division in this country is not necessarily based upon financial standing, but rather we are divided into these classes by our profession. This may seem confusing at first, but by looking at some examples it should become clearer. A person whose job it is to collect garbage may make a good income for himself (probably middle income level), but due to the nature of his job he would be considered—perceived—as being lower class. An assembly line worker may make more money than a doctor working in a clinic for the underprivileged, but the assembly worker is at best low-middle-class while the doctor is upper class. A farmer in this economically harsh time may only be making a poverty line income, but he and his family would still be classed as middle; a farmer who has somehow made the right investments and owns his own acreage and equipment may very well be in a high income bracket, but still classed "middle." Classification, then, is merely a matter of perception and open to everyone's opinion. It is not as easy as comparing incomes and then pigeonholing class distinction.

Another type of perception that occurs due to occupational roles relates to titles or positions and how we perceive those that fall into these categories. Take the position *manager*. Does it call to mind a man dressed in a three-piece suit? Someone with clean hands and a snappy professional look? In actuality, a manager could just as easily be a woman dressed in blue jeans and a T-shirt who has broken nails and calloused, dirty hands due to the requirements of her job. The point is, while we know that we "can't judge a book by its cover" or a person by her occupation, we do make initial perceptions that often keep us from viewing the real person.

I remember when I was in first grade. My mother and I were at the grocery store, and standing in the checkout line was Mrs. Slivka, my teacher. I was amazed, shocked and totally taken aback. She was buying groceries just like everybody else. This not only meant that she ate (teachers had lunch in a separate room from students at my grade school), but it probably meant she cooked, washed dishes and maybe even watched TV! I know this was a childish reaction, but then I was a child and had a child's perception of the role *teacher*. I don't know exactly why I was so affected by this—I guess I thought she lived in her desk drawer—but I know that to this day I remember how I felt when my perception proved to be wrong. Perceiving people by their title or occupation is constantly affecting how we interact and judge other people.

Another good example is the perception people hold of the role *policeman*. Most of us perceive people in law enforcement to be people we can count on in times of need. They are supposed to be fine, upstanding citizens dedicated to help citizens live in a society where crime is too often a daily fact of life. Most police officers are just such people, but think of the reaction, the perception, people have when a policeman commits a crime. We not only perceive the crime as negative, but somehow it seems worse that a law enforcer has been involved. *Doctor*, a healer, a friend, someone

to turn to when illness strikes: A person who knows about the effects of
alcohol and drug abuse, someone who could counsel an addict or alcoholic
because he *knows* what the dangers are. He is someone who would never be
involved in such abuses himself. Wrong. Our nation's perception of this
time-honored profession has recently been shocked and the AMA set back
on its heels by studies showing doctors are among the biggest mis-users of
these drugs. Perceptions based on occupations are merely that, opinions
based on beliefs that in many cases, when looked at logically and
objectively, aren't true. Certainly these perceptions indiscriminately applied
to all people who happen to have the same job are no more valid than
believing that everyone in the world finds liver to be tasty.

Sex Roles	What are little boys made of? Snips and Snails and puppy Dogs' tails, That's what little boys are Made of. What are little girls made of? Sugar and Spice and all things Nice, That's what little girls are Made of.

This quote from Robert Southey's poem "What All the World is Made of"
was written in 1820, but the perception it represents is as old as mankind
and as current as today. Men and women have always been perceived
differently due to their sex. That one single factor, being born male or
female, immediately labels and puts us into a pigeonhold that affects our
own perception, as well as the rest of the world's. Even as we approach the
dawn of a new millennium, the fact that part of the world's population has
two X chromosomes and the other part has one X and one Y chromosome is
the basis for much of the perceptual labeling and assumptions that are made
in our society. Obviously men and women are different biologically, a
physiological fact. However, most of the sex role perceptions are not based
on these biological facts, but rather on ancient societal roles. Even in the
United States where women have made great strides in equality, time
honored perceptions are still at work. Almost half of the female population
of the U.S. are involved in careers outside of the home and a large
percentage of those women are contributing to the economic survival of
themselves and their families. Old traditions, however, die slow and painful
deaths. Women, particularly those with children, are criticized for working
outside the home and have been blamed for social, moral and other causes
that have led to a decay of the traditional family in the U.S. Not only are

they often perceived this way by men and other women, but, all too often they, themselves, believe the stigma.

The daycare that my two preschoolers attend twice a week has presented me with a vivid example of how this perception works. I take my children to school and notice that several of the children are crying as their parents start to leave. I walk out into the parking lot and notice that several of the mothers have tears in their eyes. I have yet to observe a father crying because he must leave his children and go to work. This doesn't mean that fathers don't care. They do. But because of the traditional sex roles (compounded by the perception that real men don't cry) the men don't appear to suffer from the guilt as much, because working and financially supporting their families is what men are supposed to do, at least according to the acceptable male role.

This leads us to another interesting sex role perception: What is society's view of the man who stays home, takes care of the kids, cleans the house and in general supplies those services that have traditionally been "women's work"?

Males in our society have been just as misunderstood due to their sex as women have. Just because they were born male, they are expected to be stronger physically and emotionally. They are taught to suppress emotions that are deemed inappropriate for their sex and to shun close emotional ties with anyone outside their immediate family. Physical demonstrations that society accepts between two women (hugging each other, giving each other a kiss, or even holding hands) is strictly forbidden to males in the American society, lest they be labeled homosexuals and thus be perceived in a less than positive light. These behaviors that adhere to the norm are taught to children early in life. Notice a father and his young son up to the age of about five years old. It is bedtime and the father is putting his son to bed. Dad hugs him, kisses him, and wishes his son sweet dreams. Sometime within the next year or so, the scene changes to something closer to this: Dad is sitting in the living room and it's bedtime for his son. "Dad, I'm going to bed now." Dad, with a simple nod of his head replies, "Good night, son." No physical display of affection.

The standing perceptions based on sex are everywhere in our society and while massive changes have been made and social pressure eased to some extent, these perceptions that men are strong and women weak; women cry, men don't; men work outside the home and women stay at home taking care of it and their children, are still very prevalent today. They are the causes of social unrest, disagreements, and untold hurt feelings that lead to communication breakdowns.

Sex roles and occupational roles are very closely related in the perceptional process. If someone says *nurse*, what is your immediate perception of the sex of that person? You probably thought of a female even though you are aware that there are males in the profession, however, we usually label them *male nurses*. Why are *orderlies* men and *nurse's aides* female? Why refer to a *truck driver* who is a woman as a *woman truck driver*? We don't say *man truck driver*. What about *female executive*? All this labeling seems necessary to inform the listener that his or her perception of that job should not be influenced by traditional ideas about the sex of the worker. We in the U.S., are a society in transition in reference to our perception based on sex roles. Acceptable behavior by each sex is slowly changing, which should help lessen communication breakdowns caused by these perceptions. In the meantime, it is essential to realize that we make many judgments based on sexual roles and that these ideas are not necessarily correct. There is progress, however. When people are asked the first sex that comes to mind when the word *doctor* is said, over half of those responding replied that they thought of both men and women.

Having read and discussed the physiological effects and the cultural expectations that are the basis for much of our perceptions, it should be obvious that not only are there a wide range of interpretations for the same situation, but that many of these perceptions are based on factors that are either impossible to change (due to biological functions) or are so ingrained in our minds and beliefs (cultural expectation) that they are nearly as impossible to come to an agreement on as those based on physical perceptions. As stated in the first section of this chapter, the goal of learning about perception is not to get everyone to perceive everything the same. It is to firmly implant the knowledge of *why* these perceptions differ and how understanding can be achieved even when differing opinions exist. There are two more principles that apply to perception that are necessary to understand before we can advance to a method of achieving understanding.

Two Principles of Perception

1. *The perceived is a combination of itself and the perceiver.*

This principal refers to the fact that whatever is being perceived (an object, a situation, a person) is not only made up of its factual or material components, but it is also how the person viewing it sees it. Take for example a grade book. The book is not only the paper and ink that comprises its physical make-up, but also what the person seeing that grade book thinks it is. Therefore, the perception of that grade book will differ depending on how it is thought of by the person or people involved. If that book is empty, no names or grades in it, you will probably perceive it differently than a grade book that has your name in it with your grades.

This principle also answers the question of why you believe that the worn-out tennis shoes with the holes in the toes are your *best* tennies and your mother wants to throw them in the trash. Most of us have cards, programs, or ticket stubs shoved into a drawer somewhere that are of absolutely no use to anyone, but we will probably never pitch them because, to us, they aren't trash, but valuable mementos of a pleasant evening. We even have a saying that relates to this principle, "One man's trash is another man's treasure."

2. Perception is selective which involves leaving out details.

This means that when we view something (or listen to it, talk about it, etc.) we choose what it is we will pay attention to and what we will ignore. Perhaps a good paraphrase of this statement is this: we see what we want to see and hear what we want to hear. If you are listening to two people talk about the same situation, you will notice that they don't tell exactly the same tale. They were both involved in the same situation, but they didn't experience it the same way due to the selective process. This is important to remember because it explains why two or more people can be at the same place at the same time and still relate different stories.

Since anything involves an infinite amount of detail, and perception is selective, it is inevitable that in our perception of anything we will leave out numerous details. This may be due to our literal viewpoint or because a particular point, or detail, doesn't seem important or relevant to us. Suppose your task is to describe a stool that is sitting in the center of a circle surrounded by other people charged with the same task. You describe a sturdy, perfectly adequate stool. Someone sitting directly opposite you describes a broken stool. How can this be? From the other side of the circle (viewpoint), it can be seen that there is a small crack in one of the supports of the stool. This one little detail may not be very important and your lack of describing it might pass as unimportant, however, if you were describing it to someone who was going to stand on the stool to change a light bulb, your omission could be dangerous.

Leaving out details, even though you were aware of them, can also cause problems. A friend of mine hated to shop for clothes (due in part to the fact that he was 6'5" and had difficulty finding clothes to fit). He needed a suit for an upcoming occasion and asked me to look for him. He told me his size and that I should call him if I found anything. I not only found a nice (my perception) three piece suit in his size, but it was on sale! I went home, called, and gave him the information. An hour later, my friend called me back and said, "Why didn't you tell me it was pinstriped? I *hate* pinstripes!" Since he had failed to tell me about his dislike, and I had left out the fact that it was pinstriped, an argument erupted.

Keeping in mind that perception involves selection, which means leaving out details, will lessen our defensiveness when we encounter a problem caused by selective perception. This will help cut down on communication breakdowns.

You are now equipped with the basic knowledge you need to realize why people perceive things differently. Maybe you are beginning to wonder how we are able to come to any type of agreement at all. Agreements are possible, and shared perception does occur but remember, agreeing is not the most important lesson to be learned about perception.

Lessening Communication Breakdown Through Understanding

At the beginning of this chapter we stated: "The reason we need to study this phenomenon (perception) is to reduce the complications, the unnecessary arguments, hurt feelings and general misunderstandings that differences in perception often lead to."

You now are more aware of the causes of perceptual disagreements. You know their origins and hopefully realize why people interpret the same situations differently. The next step is to apply this understanding to the people you are involved with.

When a difference of opinion arises, take a moment to quickly analyze what the cause of the disagreement is. Is it a case of misunderstanding, perhaps an inefficient message was sent, or the other person isn't acquainted with all the information he needs to know? Or is it a case of physical or cultural perception at work?

Try to empathize with the other person, put yourself in his shoes, listen not only to *what* he says, but *how* he says it. Trying to understand another's point of view isn't easy. It also involves certain risks. When we open up to a set of ideas, really listening to the whys, feelings, and thoughts, we run a risk of changing our own stand on the issue. Because of this possibility, many people shy away from being empathetic, they aren't willing to take a chance. We must realize that this possibility exists, but that it is far from a certainty. Besides, taking risks, developing new ideas, and learning is the only way we grow as individuals as well as in relationships. However, we are capable and it is feasible to empathize and still not agree with the other viewpoint. Remember that the goal is to lessen the communication breakdowns that keep us from fulfilling our goals.

If you have made the decision to run the possible risks involved in truly understanding someone, the following suggestions will help you in your progress:

1. *Listen* to what the other person is saying; not just the words but how they are said. Pick up on the nonverbals as well.

2. *Be creative* as you try to understand the "whys" of what they are saying. If the speaker comes from a totally different environment than you do, use your imagination to project yourself into his position. What does it feel like?

3. *Make a firm decision* to stick to your attempts to empathize. It won't be easy trying to understand and withhold your judgment, but only through such dedication will the rewards come.

4. *Agree to disagree.* If, after thoroughly investigating the other person's perception, you still can't find a consensus to bring the different views together, let the other person know that you understand, but still don't agree with him. Don't do it in a defensive manner, but rather approach it with the attitude that he is entitled to his perception, just as you are entitled to yours.

Conclusion

And that's the bottom line: All men and women are given the ability to perceive their surroundings, selves, and relationships in a unique way. Each of us has our own opinions and perspectives. Our goal should be to reach agreements when possible through open communication. When agreement seems impossible due to physical or cultural differences in perception, then our best course of action is allowing the other person his right to believe in his perception even if we disagree. To paraphrase an old saying, "It's not who's right or wrong, but how much understanding there is." That's communication survival.

Bibliography

Dodd, Carley H. *Dynamics of Intercultural Communication.* Dubuque, Iowa: W.C. Brown, 1982.

Kelley, Harold H. *Personal Relationships: Their Structures and Processes.* Hillsdale, New Jersey: Erlbaum, 1979.

Kramarae, C. *Women and Men Speaking.* Rowley, Mass: Newbury House, 1981.

Levinson, Daniel J. *The Seasons of a Man's Life.* New York: Ballantine Books, 1978.

O'Neille, Nena and George O'Neille. *Open Marriage.* New York: M. Evans and Company, Inc. 1972.

Rubin, Zick. *Liking and Loving.* New York: Holt, Rinehart and Winston, 1973.

_____. *Children's Friendships.* Cambridge, Mass: Harvard University Press, 1980.

6

Nonverbals

I. Characteristics of nonverbals.

    A. You are always sending nonverbals.

    B. They are of an emotional nature.

    C. The nonverbal message is not understood until verified verbally.

    D. Verbal verification may not be true.

    E. Nonverbal messages are accepted over verbal ones.

II. The five areas of nonverbals.

    A. Kinesics.

    B. Proxemics.

        1. Intimate distance.

        2. Social distance.

        3. Business distance.

    C. Paralinguals.

    D. Artifacts.

    E. Environment.

Introduction

You arrive home from classes and when you enter the house, your mother is in the kitchen preparing supper. You greet her, but she doesn't respond except to slam a cupboard door. What are you likely to interpret from her behavior? This scene is an example of non-verbal communication. No verbal message has been sent except by you, but the reaction of your mother slamming the door is every bit as eloquent as if she had spoken.

So far in our discussions of communication survival we have mainly dealt with verbal messages and their interpretations, encoding and decoding, attempting to send efficient messages, and receiving those messages in the spirit in which they were delivered by the speaker. Now we shall turn our attention to a large area of communication which is just as important—nonverbal communication.

Certain studies have revealed that we can receive as much as 75% of our input from nonverbal channels: the wink, the slap, the shrug, the tone of voice. And these nonverbal messages often override or color the verbal messages. When a friend says "Good morning!", but says it in a way that makes you know he means the opposite, which message do you believe? The verbal "Good morning!" or the nonverbal tone of voice which says "Bad morning!"? If you're like most people, you will accept and integrate the nonverbal message with almost a total disregard for the verbal message. You heard what your partner said. There is no need to check further, or is there? Let's take another example and complicate it slightly.

You come into a room and see your brother. He sees you walk through the door and he leaves by the opposite door slamming it. Now, just how do you interpret his nonverbal message to you? (Suppose for the moment that your brother is not in the habit of slamming doors.) Because the door-slamming occurred when you walked in, possibly the tendency would be to believe that you were in some way to blame for the mood of your brother. He had a bone to pick with you and rather than do it right then, he just chose to register his emotions by slamming the door. You had no way of knowing that just before you walked in your brother had received a phone call cancelling his automobile insurance, and his reaction, which you took personally, had nothing to do with you. His frustration was registered by the slamming of the door, but was directed at the insurance company, not at you.

Every day we receive information from our partners and strangers by way of nonverbals they use. Our job as concerned communicators is to "read" those nonverbal signals accurately. This chapter will give you some worthwhile tools to help in your interpretations.

Characteristics of Nonverbals

First of all, let's look at some general characteristics of most nonverbals.

1. *You are always sending messages nonverbally.* Assuming you are conscious, your body is always reacting either to the world around you, or the thoughts inside your head (whether you are aware of sending messages or not!). Even when you are quietly sitting in a chair waiting for your appointment at the dentist's office, you reveal by your posture, by the use of your hands as you flip through a magazine (you may not even be consciously reading) or by the expressions of your face certain information which might be read by a sensitive observer of the scene. Sensitive public speakers are constantly aware of the effect they have on their audience by reading the nonverbal clues: the eye-contact (or lack of it), the shifting of the weight in the chairs, the audience member who repeatedly looks at his watch are signals to that speaker about how effectively his message is coming across. The audience (if asked after the lecture) may have been unaware of sending any messages whatever, but the speaker was able to pick up on a good number of body messages.

2. *The messages sent nonverbally are usually of an emotional nature.* The content of the messages we send nonverbally is emotional rather than intellectual. Ideas are difficult to transmit nonverbally, but emotions can quite easily be communicated through nonverbal channels. You might be hard pressed to explain nonverbally a subject like St. Francis of Assissi's quest for the Nature of God, but you could probably easily express the joy he felt when he discovered it. We can quickly interpret the mood our partner is expressing with no more to go on than a shrug or a glance, and the more intense the emotional tone, the easier it is to read the nonverbals (or so we think!). How can you tell when your wife is angry? What bodily clues does she exhibit? What happens to you, physically, when you become frustrated or upset? Often by tracing how emotions vent themselves in your own body, you have some clues to the signals being sent nonverbally by your partner. The frown or stern glance we got from our Sunday school

teacher when we were cutting up in church was often enough to stop the horseplay. The tone of voice of the boss when she was chewing you out is a clue so strong that you can't ignore it. However, we must remember that no nonverbal is really interpreted accurately until the nonverbal signals have been verified verbally.

3. *You may wish to clarify verbally your interpretation of a nonverbal you have observed.* An exercise that has proven to be an eye-opener to many of our students is this one: They are asked to go out from the class and observe two people. One is to be a person who is close to them; the other, a stranger. They are to describe a nonverbal they see the person use, interpret what they think the nonverbal is saying, and then check with the person verbally to see if their interpretation is accurate. One may see a fellow in the cafeteria with his chin resting on his hand, with slumped shoulders, staring off into space ignoring the cup of coffee before him. What is this person's body telling the observer? Perhaps his slumped shoulders seem to be telling you that he did poorly on a test. You ask him if he did as poorly as you fear you did. He responds that he wasn't even thinking about the test you both just took, but rather about the date he had scheduled for the weekend. We'll discuss later how much credence we can place on the verbal verification. For this exercise it is enough that you tried to clarify your interpretation by checking the source of the nonverbal.

4. *Verbal verification of a nonverbal may not be true.* A nonverbal which you attempt to verify verbally may not be "verified." In other words, when we interpret a nonverbal response and then present the explanation to the person whose behavior we have observed asking her if this is what she meant, her reply may not be an honest one. Since our actions speak louder (and more truthfully) than our words, we often tend to deny what our bodies are saying. The reason for this is simply that we are using a defense mechanism. We say one thing verbally, but our nonverbals express the opposite. In order to overcome these conflicting statements we may, when asked for verification of our nonverbal message, deny its statement and reiterate with the verbal denial. One woman in class asked her husband if he would help her study definitions for an up-coming test (he would check her notes to see if she was identifying the terms correctly). He rolled his eyes and heaved a large sigh. She interpreted his gestures to mean that he would rather watch the football game on TV and not help her with her definitions. When she asked him point-blank if that was what he meant to convey, he denied that the gesture meant that he wouldn't help her. The class suggested that although she had attempted verification by verbal means, her partner had lied to her. One thing we must realize about verbal communication is that it takes more cerebral effort than nonverbal communication and

consequently there is more time and opportunity for subterfuge. Most of us have more practice at "controlling" our verbal messages. We have trained (and been trained) from an early age to develop "proper," "acceptable" verbal responses, even when these responses are in direct conflict with our feelings. Our nonverbal responses, however, have not been honed as carefully, and therefore we can "cloud" a message verbally as easily as we can "clarify" that same message.

5.*Nonverbals are accepted over verbal messages.* Perhaps because we learned nonverbals first, we tend to read and accept the nonverbal message even when it contradicts a verbal message. Our partner says "Nothing's wrong!" so loudly and defensively we *know* something *is* wrong. We just don't know how much we're to blame.

Now that we have discussed some of the characteristics of nonverbal communication, here are some areas in which this kind of communication is used.

Areas of Nonverbal Communication

Kinesics. The area of nonverbal communication which is the most visable is called *kinesics.* It covers what we might call "body language": (1) the expressions on the face, (2) the gestures of the hands, (3) the posture of the body. As we achieve consciousness every morning, we become aware of the actions of our body: the growl of the stomach wanting breakfast, the stiff neck needing a good stretch to relieve tension, the bruised knee needing a rub to get the blood flowing. As we step out of bed, swinging ourselves to an upright position, we become aware of our head, our eyes, our sinuses, etc. From the moment we are conscious we begin sending nonverbal messages, some on purpose, many unconsciously, but we are still saying something with posture and expression.

1. Expressions of the face: Think back to the times you have observed and interpreted kinesic action: The smile and wink from that attractive person across the room from you in Math. The teenager jumping off the school bus leap-frogging the first three mailboxes trying to impress the girl who followed him off the bus. Your father's expression behind his evening paper when you asked if you could borrow the car. The vocabulary of kinesics is something you learned as a very small child. In fact, it is probably the first "language" you learned, long before actual language and words made any sense to you. But note the variety possible in an expression so thoroughly understood as a smile. This simple, familiar expression may include the shy, timid look of a child seeing Santa Claus for the first time

and range all the way to the bawdy sneer of a drunk who just heard (or told) a dirty story at the neighborhood tavern. Such variety is possible and yet we assume that our partners will know precisely how to interpret the shade of meaning they see on our faces. Watch a mother attempt to feed an infant in a high chair. Her mouth will form the very contortions which she wishes the child to perform as she is feeding her. The mother opens her own mouth and expresses with her tongue the very actions which she wishes her child to perform with the baby food. Or, notice someone administer disinfectant to a cut for a friend or relative. The person who is doing the doctoring will very often screw up her face into a terrible scowl of pain even though she will not be the one experiencing the sting of the antiseptic.

Expressions can tell us much, but are only part of the picture of kinesics.

2. Hands. While we in the Western cultures do not place the emphasis on gestures which our counterparts do in the areas of the Middle East or the Orient, we still can learn a great deal about the person we are observing by how he manipulates his hands. When we see someone who has crossed his arms and kept his fists clenched under his arms, we have a pretty good idea

that this person is in a "closed" position: Mind made up, not about to change his opinion easily. Viewing a person who is "open" with arms and palm extended to us gives us an opposite impression: one of acceptance and concern. Perhaps you are a "pocket" person with hands often jammed in pants or jacket pockets. This gesture can mean you are trying to keep warm, or that you are somewhat guarded and have not quite made up your mind about a given idea or proposition. While hands are important to watch, they must be seen in relation with both the expressions on the face and the posture of the body.

3. Posture. This area of kinesics takes in the body as a whole: the set of the shoulders, the slump of the torso, the positioning of the legs and feet. These actions are observable and readable given some clue about the surrounding events. Glance around at the posture of the people sitting and listening to the next lecture in class. What are they telling you and the lecturer by their various postures? Remember that posture may not give you much information. The interpretation may need to include observation of the expressions on the face, the working of the hands as well as the posture of the body.

Proxemics. Along with the position of the body we should investigate the juxtaposition (distancing) of the body with others. What is the spacial relationship? The distance and height relationship of one person to another is often very significant in explaining, without saying a word, the quality and substance of the social relationship between the two people. Artists have been aware of this spacial message and are able to indicate in a family portrait who has the power in the family by the way the other figures are placed in relationship to either Mama or Papa.

One of the delights of my teaching has been to invite guest lecturers to speak to my classes. A budding graduate student came to my class one night to give a lecture on proxemics and did it this way: He felt that the best way to illustrate what he was describing was to do it as he talked about other things. So while he defined what "proxemics" was and who had researched the topic, he began to illustrate his topic. He sat on the edge of the desk. He moved close to one of the girls in the class. He walked around behind the desk and crouched behind the desk. He even jumped up on top of the desk which convinced some of the students that he had, indeed, lost his mind. What was marvelous about the demonstration, though, was that the class never forgot the picture in their minds of his lecturing to them from the top of the desk in the front of the room, his head so close to the florescent light fixture. What do we tell people by the ways we use "proxemics"?

Have you ever had a date with a person who kept himself far away from you all evening? In the car he was sitting as close to the opposite door as

possible. At the restaurant he took the seat across the table rather than the one closest around the corner. What was he saying nonverbally? It could be a number of things, but one thing is pretty certain—he doesn't trust you. We work our messages from three main distances.

1. The intimate distance (from our skin out to about three feet). In this space we allow only our most intimate family members and our closest friends. You may have heard it referred to as your "personal bubble." The only time we let strangers into this circle is when we must for practical reasons—the elevator, the street corner, the bus or subway. In such places we very carefully meet the eyes of the stranger and then look away as if to say: "I'm sorry, I don't like this anymore than you do, but we both must be on this vehicle."

2. Social distance: (about 3 feet to about 5 feet), the distance at which we can carry on a casual conversation. This is the distance that chairs and couches are positioned in most living and family rooms. It is a comfortable space—not too close nor too far away.

3. Business distance—(five to ten feet). This is the distance at which most transactions involving money, hiring and firing, interviews, or non-personal matters are dealt with. Notice where the chairs are placed in the office of the President of your bank. Her chair may be directly behind the desk. When you enter the room to ask for a loan, she may rise or not; that is her

prerogative. The chair she indicates for you will probably be five to ten feet from her own. Notice also that she is "protected" by the barrier of the desk. All these symbols of authority (her own office, her desk, her chair, and the relationship of her chair to yours) are nonverbal, but they speak very loudly in determining for you just what sort of a relationship you are going to have with this person. This business distance is also the area involved when you order food from a fast-food restaurant versus the closer distance of the waiter at a finer restaurant. Kinesics and proxemics, then, form a very large and loud section of our non-verbal communications.

Paralinguals. This area of nonverbals concerns the sounds we make which are apart from language: the grunts, the sighs, the moans. This area of nonverbals also includes the tone of voice produced by volume, pitch, and speed of delivery. We learn very quickly how to say one thing and mean another. Sarcasm is based upon the tone of voice. The simple phrase "Oh! what a lovely dress!" in the mouth of a sarcastic hostess can do much to destroy the confidence of one of her guests. A boy was asked by a friend if he had gotten permission for the campout. The boy replied, "They said 'maybe.'" His friend then asked, "was it a 'no-maybe' or a 'yes-maybe'?"

We all learn to judge the negative or positive values of our parent's communication with us. Often this comes in the tone of voice. Think back to a time you were spanked. Unless your parents were most "modern" in their thinking, you probably can remember what led up to the spanking, the kinds of things which were said by your parents to justify the punishment. My guess is also that you can remember most of all the authoritarian tone of voice used by Mother or Father which preceded the actual "laying on of hands." My niece was at my house one day and got into trouble with her grandmother who was just ready to spank the child when the girl turned to her and said "Grandma, don't use your 'school teacher' voice!" My mother, rather than punishing the girl, burst out laughing and confessed to me later that whenever she had to "give us a licking" she tried to sound in control by using what the little girl had identified as her "school teacher voice."

Artifacts. This area of nonverbals includes messages we send, consciously or unconsciously, by the clothes we wear, the hair-style we prefer, the jewelry and accessories we choose. Now, please avoid becoming defensive at this point; I very often ask a class to cast their eyes around the room to see the shoes that are worn by their fellow students. What messages are those people sending about their feet? Their sense of style or fashion? Their income? These messages, just like so much nonverbal information we think we can interpret accurately, may not tell the whole story about a person. There was a grand woman in her late sixties who was a family friend I remember who could spend literally hundreds of dollars for an outfit only to wind up looking like something the cat dragged in. Clothes were not important to her. But one had to overlook her attire to get to know the woman as a person before one could appreciate what she was.

Notice how your friends handle their coffee cup, their beer bottle, their cigarette. One friend has suggested that I handle a martini glass as if I were making love to it! This was an area of my nonverbals that I was totally unaware of. But to at least one person, my friend, a message was being sent. Notice the actors in period plays and the way they use their costume or props to reveal the core of their character. One example of this is a scene in Moliere's *The Misanthrope* in a production that I saw at the University of Iowa. The character, Arsinoé, is having a quarrel with Alceste's sweetheart, Celemene, in the second act of the play. The two women are really scrapping and after every barb Arsinoé threw she reached for a mint from a little tin box she carried for the scene. Mean as she was, she wished to give the impression that she was just as sweet as the mints she was eating. The director had seized upon a very simple way of emphasizing the duplicity of her character by the use of a prop carried by the actress.

Since the days of Haight-Ashbury in San Francisco and the flower children of the 60's men have been free to choose long hair styles without fearing that their masculinity would be questioned. Earrings, too, once the exclusive property of woman, are being sported by the masculine gender, also. A number of articles of apparel once thought to belong to one sex or the other are now worn by both without regard to a specific sexual statement. Apart, then, from a statement of fashion consciousness, what can clothes reveal nonverbally?

Artifacts may give some indication of the economic status of the individual. Some people are inveterate "label readers." But you can never be quite sure if this message is always complete, either. There used to be a gag in Dallas about the oil millionaires taking their wives to the Dallas Civic Opera: she would be dressed in the latest fashion from Nieman-Marcus and he would be in a simple blue serge suit with a white Stetson cowboy hat. The oil man could have spent a mint on his suit, but preferred the simple attire. Sometimes label-readers can be mistaken.

You might be able to guess about the cleanliness habits of the individual (if you can get close enough). But here, too, you may be out of luck. Certain medicines may react with some people's body chemistry in such a way as to give off an odor which might be misconstrued to indicate a lack of proper hygiene when the condition may really be something else entirely.

This matter of "artifacts" may give messages, but the careful communicator must be certain to verify those messages through other means.

Environment. This is the last area of nonverbals which may give us some information. Here we are interested in the message given by inanimate objects: the work place, the home, the restaurant, and the hospital.

Let's begin by taking a look around your classroom. Suppose you were given an unlimited budget, how would you redecorate the room to more thoroughly place the students at ease and encourage more individuals to participate in discussion? The "institutional beige" walls might be painted another color; the bare walls might be decked out with pictures or posters; the chairs might be replaced with recliners or pillows; and some quiet, lulling music might begin and end a class session. Perhaps you would replace the glaring florescent lights with area lamps and add some potted plants or blooming flowers to soften the start lines of the room. These are some of the suggestions we have received about our classroom from students who would like to attempt some "statement" about the environment in which they pursue the study of communication.

Look at the restaurants you frequent. What are some of the differences between the fast-food places you "grab a snack", and the more expensive restaurants where you "dine"? The first is geared to the philosophy of volume in business: "get 'em in and get 'em out." The second is more concerned with the atmosphere which will encourage you to stay and enjoy or savor a meal. The chairs in the second type of restaurant are more comfortable; the carpet is thicker (reducing table clatter and conversational noise); the colors used in the decor are more subtle; even the people waiting

tables in the second type of restaurant are less hurried, more refined, quieter — all indications of an attempt on the part of the establishment to create an atmosphere which induces relaxation and encourages digestion.

Studies conducted about the work place have indicated that the efficiency of the workers can be improved by some attention to their surroundings. Large corporations with countless secretaries (of both sexes) have found that inexpensive panel walls cutting up the space in large rooms with endless desks and typewriters can give the workers a feeling of privacy, and hence, pride in their work in addition to reducing the noise factor of the clattering phones and typewriters. Providing workers with physical activity areas, saunas, jogging tracks, and volleyball courts reduces stress on the individual worker and heightens efficiency.

Which is your favorite room in your home? Why? What is there about the decor or the surroundings in that room which make you feel good? The factor of environment can play a large part in communication if we become aware of it, and consciously work to place ourselves in an environment which "works" for us.

Conclusion

Nonverbal communication covers a large part of our conscious and unconscious communication. Messages sent by our body we can attempt to control, but our bodies may "give us away" even so. The messages are generally of an emotional nature and cannot be trusted until we verify those messages we think we have gotten. Even with verbal verification, our partners may still not be sending efficient messages and we must constantly fight the tendency to "read something into" what we observe. Skilled as we think we are at knowing the vocabulary of body language which we have seen our partners use, we must treat each communication experience as a new one. Our partners need to be given the opportunity of responding in a spontaneous fashion, the same opportunity we expect for ourselves — behaving in each situation like the unique individual we believe ourselves to be.

Bibliography

Birdwhistell, Ray L. *Kinesics and Context.* Philadelphia: University of Pennsylvania Press, 1970.

David Flora. *Inside Intuition; What we Know About Nonverbal Communication.* New York: McGraw-Hill Book Co., 1973.

Dodd, Charley H. *Dynamics of Intercultural Communication.* Dubuque, Iowa: W.C. Brown, 1982.

Ekman, Paul and Wallace V. Friesen. *Face to Face.* Englewood Cliffs, New Jersey: Prentice-Hall, 1975.

Mehrabian, Albert. *Silent Messages.* 2nd Ed. Belmont, California: Wadsworth, 1981.

7

Semantics

I. Three characteristics of language.
   A. Language is convenient.
   B. Language contains two levels of meaning.
      1. Denotative.
      2. Connotative.
   C. Language can confuse as well as clarify.

II. Kinds of language that confuse.
   A. Ambiguity.
   B. Abstractions.
   C. Euphemisms.
   D. Emotionally-charged words.

III. Suggestions to clarify language communication.
   A. Observe your delivery.
   B. Choose words accurately.
   C. Know your partner.
   D. Consider the length of the exchange.

Introduction

Sure, if I reprehend anything in this world it is the use of my oracular tongue, and nice derangement of epitaphs.

Mrs. Malaprop from *The Rivals*
by Richard Brindley Sheridan.

Why is Mrs. Malaprop amusing to us? Perhaps because she reminds us of situations when we ourselves chose a wrong word to express ourselves. Since we've all experienced the embarrassment of misusing words with various results, it seems necessary to address this common problem. Is it as simple as choosing an appropriate word or group of words so that our messages will be received accurately? Not necessarily. In choosing words we think thoroughly and adequately express our ideas, we have only covered part of the problem of communication as it relates to language. We also need to be certain that the words we choose are understood by the partner to whom we speak. How can we be certain? How can we guess just how a term or phrase will affect our partners? How can we clarify our thinking and, hence, our communication? These will be questions we shall answer as we discuss the area of communication called "semantics," the study of word usage.

Characteristics of Language

The Convenience of Language

What is language? It is certain sounds we utter and a complex set of symbols which stands for ideas and objects. Therefore, language is convenient. It allows us to communicate with others who speak the same language. Yet, we know that messages sent aren't necessarily the messages received. Our choice of words is not always effective in its results. Is there any other way of communicating which might be more efficient? Suppose for a day we were to carry around pictures which would clearly show everything we wished to talk about during that day. We could pull out a picture using it to literally speak for us. We'd have to have a very large satchel to carry pictures of everything we wished to talk about! Also, what if something happened and we did not have a certain picture to express our thoughts? Would that mean that we could not talk about it? Language is convenient. We carry in our heads a list of words we call a vocabulary, and from this list of thousands of words we choose the ones which will express what we wish our partners to know. We play a game of "mix and match." If we are careless about the words we pick, then our partner may not perceive our message correctly, and the exchange for which language was created (making communication convenient) would become a barrier to understanding, thus creating loss of time and maybe even tempers.

The Levels of Meaning in Language

Connotations and Denotations

One problem we face with the use of language is that the meanings of words are comprised of both connotative and denotative levels of definition. Take the words "child," for example. If I were to ask you to define the word, you might say something like this: A "child" is a young person roughly between the ages of one and twelve years old." You have given a "denotive" definition, then. You have explained what the word means generally, or in most contexts. But there is another quality to the word "child," isn't there? Another level of meaning? When we use the term "child," we might also imply that the individual we speak of has a certain quality of innocence, that he is immature, that he speaks his mind without bias or worry of offending (as we often see children do!). These other levels of meaning of the word are what we call "connotative": that is, the cluster of feelings and images which surround a word we use which often means as much as the denotation of the word.

Another word we might explore is "snow." We know intellectually that "snow" is H_2O, a crystalized form of water. But what else does the word mean to us? Bad driving conditions, warm fireplaces, popcorn and cocoa, Christmas, heavy winter clothing, skiing? All these other images cluster around the one word, "snow."

Observe how poets use connotations as well as denotations to strengthen their creations. Poetry, we say, is "distilled discourse." It is made more effective by the use poets make of words which mean more than themselves, calling up images above and beyond the actual word on the page. When John Keats, in "*The Eve of St. Agnes,*" talks about Madeline's gown that "creeps rustling to her knees:...," he is not just describing a girl getting ready for bed. He has given the gown a sound. Rich brocade would make just such a sound. He has recreated in our ears as well as our eyes the picture of that incident on St. Agnes's Eve.

Our job, then, as communicators is to choose the word which not only expresses our thoughts accurately (denotation), but which will carry to our listener the feelings and images we wish them to receive (connotation).

The Possible Confusions of Language

Language can cloud as well as reveal. I suspect that we were not very old when we first learned to "hedge" an issue, using words to distract or confuse rather than clarify our meanings. When our mothers ask us "What's going on in there?" what was our response? "Nothing, Mom!" and being the wise mother she was, she came on the run to see just what mischief we had created. As we grow older, we learn more subtle ways to "cover our tracks." We delay, we prevaricate, we plead—all ways of using language to cloud communication.

The realm of politics is a great place to observe the person who can answer a question without ever giving a straight answer. When asked if we are provoking an enemy of our country, our president might say "Our aim is to create an atmosphere for world peace." And who could fault him? Isn't "world peace" a grand and noble goal? But, he never answered the reporter's question. He never said "Yes" or "No" to the question asked.

Recall the rhetoric that surrounded the Viet Nam War. The commanders were using words like "troop strength" when they really meant "troop weakness." They referred to "assault maneuvers" when they really meant "retreat." Part of the frustration of the American public during that conflict stemmed from the undeniable fact that we were being lied to regarding the actions of our forces in that remote part of the world. Language was used as a barrier to truth.

In our own relationships we very quickly learn what to say and what not to say, what things will make our partners worry, or upset, or hostile. Language can be a weapon. Think back upon the last time you had a fight with your closest friend. Was the misunderstanding based upon a word or phrase you used which was misinterpreted by your partner? We used to chant on the playground: "Sticks and stones may break my bones, but words can never hurt me!" But we were wrong! Words *can* hurt, and often we know just which words to use which will hurt the most.

Language, then, for all its convenience and its versatility can be powerful when used as a weapon. But when we use language in that way, we must learn to pay the consequences in lost friendships and hurt feelings on the part of our partners. This damage will have to be repaired if we are to re-establish clear and honest communication.

Language "Hang-Ups"

Ambiguity. Part of the problem of communication, as it regards language, is that we choose the wrong (or in someways deceptive) word to express our ideas. Consequently, when the partner hears or reads our thought, he gets an entirely different idea than the one we intended. As a teacher, I have often run across this problem as it pertains to writing test questions. A recent example of this was a quiz I gave for a course in Oral Interpretation of Literature which covered our discussions of the 18th century Augustan poets. I had included in my lectures of this era certain details about the life-styles of this period, and had attempted to relate the ornate decoration of individuals and their surroundings to the careful structure of the poetry which we covered. My question was this: "Pick an Augustan poet and describe how his poetry reflected his age." After the quiz a student came to me and said, "But you never told us the ages of the poets as they were writing." I responded, "Huh?" He went on to discuss how he had answered the question by assuming Alexander Pope was in his early twenties when he wrote "Rape of the Lock." Finally, I began to see the light. He had interpreted "his age" to refer to the actual chronological age of the poet while I had intended to imply that "his age" meant the entire era in which the poet lived. The student had a very legitimate gripe. I couldn't fault the answer. (Actually, I now see that I could have capitalized Age and some of the confusion would have been avoided.) But the ambiguity existed despite my sincere attempt to place clear, concise questions on the exam.

Another example occurred when I received an invitation through the mail to attend a party. The invitation stated that the dress was to be "informal." My date and I discussed the question and "informal" meant sport coat and slacks for me and a simple cocktail dress for her. We arrived to find we were the only ones who had not worn blue jeans. Our host was some fifteen years our junior and had used a word which he thought would be self-explanatory. I had not thought to check with him about a further explanation. Needless to say we felt just a little over-dressed for the occasion.

Ambiguity strikes again! A phrase or word which can be taken two ways resulted in two misunderstandings. How easily both of the problems could have been overcome had word choice been clearer, or had the interpretation of the word been questioned.

Abstractions. Here we approach an area in which the word chosen is appropriate enough, but is not specific enough. If I tell you that I have a "friend" you have some information: You do not know which sex this friend is; you do not know how close our relationship is; you do not know how old my friend is. Suppose I tell you that I know a "person who teaches." Again, you have some information, but only about that person's occupation, and that I am acquainted with him/her. If, however, I say "My friend, Bill, teaches with me." you know the sex, occupation, sort of relationship, and approximate age of the person of whom I am speaking.

S. I. Hayakawa has created what he terms an "abstraction ladder" which can be used to describe people, events, or objects. At the foot of the ladder one is on a clear, solid foundation of specifics: Randy, my brown springer spaniel puppy; Susie, my 18-month-old niece; my high school senior prom (c. 1955). As one climbs the ladder of abstraction, the events, people, and objects get more and more obscure to the point that you are speaking vaguely about my pet, my relative, a dance. In the cloudy world of abstractions no one will be able to sue for what you say, but the power of your speech will be lost.

Obviously, avoiding abstractions altogether is very time-consuming, but I remind you here of one of our assumptions as we began this text: Communication takes time. If it's worth doing, it is worth doing well, completely, specifically, and clearly.

Euphemisms. There are words that are delicate. In the days before the sexual revolution, say the 1950's, a term which was often used to describe a woman who was going to have a baby was that she was in a "delicate condition." Unless you knew the woman very well, no one of any taste or cultural background would consider using so strong (and accurate a term) as "pregnant." This is just one example of the use of a "euphemism," a word which softens the actual event or function being described. Such language choice has been in fashion as long as we have had language. One does not refer to someone "dying"; they "pass away." A proper British matron would never ask for directions to a "rest room" or "toilet"; she asks "Where may I wash?" No one would object to such obviously subtle and refined descriptions. The reason I bring the subject up here is that occasionally we can get carried away in our attempt to spare feelings, and discuss our ideas in terms which become so vague and sterile that the purpose of the discussion is lost. Oscar Wilde in his delightful spoof of Victorian society, *The Importance of Being Ernest,* introduces a country girl, Cecily. In the "Tea scene" between Cecily and a somewhat older woman, Gwendolyn from London high society, the playwright in order to emphasize the simple, straightforward nature of Cecily has her state: "When I see a spade, I call it a spade!" To which Gwendolyn replies: "I'm glad to say I have never seen a spade. It is obvious our social spheres are widely different."

When we wish to discuss a point with our partner, it is essential that the discussion remain on a plane which will be mutually recognizable and not lost in the haze of misdirected refinement. Again, the choice of words needs to be clear, accurate, and, yes, even blunt to avoid misunderstandings and perhaps hurt feelings. (See Appendix for "Weasel-Worders think Softer Speech is Safer Speech.")

Emotionally-Loaded Words. These are words which carry considerably more than their own weight when discussions arise, and are chosen often to divert the discussion from the subject at hand to another, more satisfactory or agreeable one. We all know what things we can say to get under the skin of our partners and what is important here is not so much which word is chosen as the effect that it may have. The politician's "flag-waving" speech is an example. The use of inference rather than direct statement. Archie Bunker's "pinko, Commie, fag" line. All use the words which will in their connotations, call up the desired response in the audience or partner. What words set your mind reeling? We do not mean the four-letter variety, without which some people could not speak at all, but refer to those terms which upon hearing you find it difficult to "keep your cool."

A friend of mine uses a perfectly innocuously sounding word: growth. When she uses it in referring to our relationship ("I think our relationship needs more growth"), I know exactly what she means. She means that I am behaving in an immature fashion and that *I'm* the one who needs to "grow." Now, I know full well that the word is a perfectly good one, accurate and clear. But, when it is used in this context, I see red! We have

discussed my reaction to the word, and she has ceased to use it. She had no idea that it struck me so very wrong.

In choosing the words to express ourselves we need to try to avoid the abstract, ambiguous, euphemistic, and emotionally-charged phrases which tend to shut our partner out, or make him defensive so that communication can continue and the exchange be enhanced with feedback. I do not want to leave the impression that communication should be without emotion. What human contact is rewarding without it? But without destructive emotion brought on by language choice, greater understanding and mutual needs can be attained.

Having covered the examples of the ways in which words can "go astray" in our communication, we now reach the point where we can offer some suggestions which may ameliorate some of the difficulties faced by the person interested in clarity of expression.

Clarity of Delivery. No matter how carefully we choose the words we use for our expression, no matter how conscientious we are about determining the effects of language on our partners; if the presentation of the message in terms of vocal delivery is garbled, the message stands little chance of being received. If you are a mumbler, one who does not pronounce words clearly or does not enunciate the syllables accurately, your message may be lost. How often have you asked a friend to repeat a comment because he failed to speak distinctly? The request to repeat is doubly frustrating: it frustrates the speaker and the listener. Clarify your presentation of even simple exchanges like a request for help in a store. Get into the habit of speaking distinctly and when you reach those exchanges which are emotionally charged or threatening, you will find that the clarity of delivery will keep the attention on the message, not the presentation of that message.

Clarity of Word Choice. Learn words. Become familiar with your language. Attempt to choose the proper word for the situation and your use of "you know what I mean" will diminish. One of the most frequently asked questions we get as teachers is "How can I enlarge my vocabulary?" Nothing could be easier. But the process does take some discipline. You must read. Newspapers, magazines, novels—all provide you with words used in usually accurate ways. Become aware of the ways others use the language and emulate those whom you respect. Each day in your classes you are subjected to a variety of teachers and thus a variety of vocabularies. As you take notes, keep track of the words which are unfamiliar to you. Ask questions about words which are unfamiliar (after class is best). This will be a big step toward a more enlarged and useful vocabulary. And, yes, use the dictionary. Remember it is only a book. It cannot bite! It can become a familiar tool to help you expand your thinking and your thought processes.

Clarity of Understanding of Your Partner. Along with the work on the vocabulary, be aware that we have already suggested that your partner is really the true test of the accuracy of your message delivery: Does what I am saying get through to my partner? To answer this complex question you need to be sensitive to the needs of others as well as your own. You will need to be aware of the nonverbals used which indicate the appropriate time for certain exchanges. Watch for the signs of frustration, fatigue, happiness in your partners and you will have a very good measure of the kind of communication your partner will be likely to accept. To a large extent, meanings are in people, not just in words.

Clarity in Choosing the Appropriate Length for Exchange. In an English class many years ago I was told "Verbiage rhymes with garbage. Make your sentence only as long as you have meaning to sustain it." We all hate the "blow-hard", that person who talks just to be talking regardless of whether or not he has anything to say. To avoid this label, understand that certain exchanges have certain expectations as far as your partners are concerned. A simple request for the time of day need not take the whole afternoon. On the other hand, a request from your partner to share a problem with you will probably take more than five minutes. Common sense will dictate the variations to you, so keep alert.

Conclusion

To make yourself understood in this or any language you need precisely the same skills you need to be a good listener: understanding and sensitivity both to the partner and the language you choose to use.

Bibliography

Chase, Stuart. *Power of Words.* New York: Harcourt, Brace and Co., 1954.

DeVito, Joseph A. *Language: Concepts and Processes.* Englewood Cliffs, New Jersey: Prentice-Hall, 1973.

Farb, Peter. *Word Play (What Happens When People Talk?).* New York: Alfred A. Knopf, Inc., 1973.

Hayakawa, S.E. *Language and Thought in Action.* New York: Harcourt Brace Javanovich, 1964.

Miller, George A. and Philip N. Johnson-Laird. *Language and Perception.* Cambridge, Mass: The Belknap Press, 1976.

Narisco, John and David Burkett. *Declare Yourself.* Englewood Cliffs, New Jersey: Prentice-Hall, 1975.

8

Conflict
Resolution

I. Conflict can be defined as a difference of opinion.

   A. Conflicts produce emotions in both parties.
   B. Each person has a "personal stake" in the outcome.

II. Conflicts grow from a "flower of evil."

   A. The atmosphere is extremely charged.
   B. The "personal stake" can lead away from a solution.
   C. There is a possibility of a power struggle.

III. The four postures in conflict.

   A. Non-assertive behavior.
   B. Aggression.
   C. Passive-aggression.
   D. Assertive behavior.

IV. Ways to resolve conflicts.

   A. Set up the atmosphere for resolution.
   B. Keep to one problem.
   C. Be sensitive to your partner's needs.
   D. Develop your own plan for resolution.

Introduction

If you could wave a magic wand and remove all conflict from your life, would you? Before you answer this question think for a moment about what conflict adds to your life. Think of the stimulation you receive from a healthy exchange of feelings on a baseball diamond. Remember the heart-stopping dread you felt when your partner told you she never wanted to see you again. Recall the sometimes heated exchanges you have had with your boss or fellow-worker regarding the best work procedure to use.

Conflict Defined

As human beings we experience emotions. Often we exhibit those emotions to those around us. We feel and we show what we feel. The times we are likely to become most emotional are when we are faced with a conflict which we'll define as a difference of opinion between people on any issue. "Conflict" may be regarded as a blanket term covering anything from a slight disagreement over what to have for supper all the way to war. Most of the conflicts we face in our lives fall somewhere in between these two extremes: We quarrel with a roommate about whose turn it is to take out the trash or vacuum the rug. We fight with our parents about curfew. We question a professor about a grade on a test. These situations are potential conflicts which we must meet and solve. Our survival as capable individuals depends upon how successfully we are able to resolve these conflicts we face. Let us look at these situations just mentioned to see what qualities they share in common.

1. They all produce emotions in both people.
2. Each person has a personal stake in the outcome.
3. Each can result in a struggle for power of one partner *over* the other.

In a minute we'll look at each quality and see how it contributes to the potentially volatile situation we call "conflict." But first, let's see how conflicts arise in the first place between individuals.

Flower of Evil

Imagine that the conflict (whatever it is) begins from a small flower. Let's call this flower a "flower of evil." It grows slowly and puts out one petal at a time, each petal representing a gripe you have with your partner. Simple things, all of them. Not enough to jump on your partner for at the time, just something he does that is irritating. He clears his throat in an odd way. He never fills the ice-cube tray. She hangs her panty hose over the shower rod to dry. Each irritation adds another petal to the flower of evil until suddenly you have a full-blown conflict. In *The Odd Couple* Oscar tells Felix "I have a list of the ten things you do that drive me crazy!" Now, that's a good example of a full-blown "flower of evil"! The reason we need to be aware of this flower's growth is that once it blooms, something quite inconsequential may trigger a real blow up on our part which leaves our partner bewildered because he may be unaware of the build up. To us (aware of all the events leading to the confrontation) it seems a major conflict; to our partner it may seem we are making "a mountain out of a mole hill." Now that we have seen how conflicts develop, let's investigate three qualities most conflicts share.

Emotion in Conflict. When we are in a conflict or fight, we often are dealing in an atmosphere of excessive emotion. All the stops are pulled-out. We are fighting for our positive self-concept (almost as if we were fighting for our lives!) We are defensive. Our hearts beat faster; we sweat; we raise our voices or increase the rate of our speech. This highly emotional state we find ourselves in is not very conducive to finding reasonable solutions. We need to let ourselves "cool off" before we again approach our partner in order to find a rational solution to the problem.

Personal Stake in the Conflict. One of the reasons we become so emotional is that we feel we have a personal stake in the outcome of the conflict. We identify so strongly with the problem that we find it difficult to be rational or objective: my mother attacks me for being thoughtless. She may say something like "You were really thoughtless about not calling to tell me you'd be late for supper." She has made a specific accusation. Along with the specific information, she has generalized the criticism to include a blanket statement about my personality. My self image is under attack and I will feel the need to defend my actions, regardless of the fact that I cannot turn back the clock and undo what has already been done. If I do not wish to be perceived as "thoughtless" by my mother (and I obviously do not), I may waste valuable time explaining and defending past actions rather than focusing attention on the future and a solution. My "personal stake" is with the problem, not the solution. My act of defending is wasted effort, energy that could better be used in a constructive way.

Power Struggle. Additional wasted effort goes into something which often occurs in conflict and that is a power struggle: an attempt on the part of one party in the conflict to exercise power over the other one. If I can just get my partner to give in to me, *I* can solve the problem. This idea is erroneous for this reason. The conflict exists between *two* people, and consequently its solution must also include input from *both* individuals. Even if power could be gained by one party who then attempted to force a solution upon his partner, the solution would be unilateral and, hence, unsatisfactory as far as the weaker partner is concerned.

Another drawback is evident with the "power struggle" solution. Suppose I am able to gain power over my partner and affect *my* solution. My partner will be less inclined to make the solution work because she still harbors resentment over the "power struggle," and because she has had no input regarding the solution, she may be less inclined to put that solution into effect.

Say my wife and I are at odds about disciplining our daughter. I feel the child should be grounded for coming in later than she had said she would from a recent party. My wife feels that I am being overly harsh. I think, mistakenly, that if my wife gives in to me, then I can discipline the daughter and all will be well. But, my carrying out a punishment which my wife believes unjust and harsh does not in any way minimize the conflict between her and me. Even though I get my wife to concede to my viewpoint, we have not found a "solution" to the problem of punishment which is mutually satisfactory. The power struggle is irrelevant to solving the conflict. Note what I am then stuck with as a result of "winning" the power struggle: one unhappy daughter and one resentful wife. Why can't my wife and I find a mutually acceptable solution regarding our daughter? The answer may lie in the ways we fight: our behavior in the tense arena of conflict.

Four Basic Behaviors in Interpersonal Communication

When faced with a situation which we feel threatening to our reputation, self-esteem, or professional standing, we tend to react in four different ways: 1) Non-assertive, 2) Aggressive, 3) Passive aggressive, or 4) Assertive. We'll look at each of these behaviors and discuss the probable outcomes as we follow each of them.

Non-Assertive Behavior. This behavior is what I like to call the "doormat-of-the-world" behavior, the stance which allows any and everybody to walk all over you without really putting up any kind of defense or struggle at all. Perhaps you have a favorite aunt or friend who reacts this way to any conflict she faces. Rather than "make a big deal" of the situation, she simply acquieses and allows whoever to have his/her own way in the matter. The non-assertive type of individual may be depended upon to "go along with the gang", matching her desires to those of the group to the point of being taken advantage of only because it seems easier at the time. Let's look at the non-assertive person in action: There is a rock concert and the non-assertive person has been chosen to get a block of tickets and then presumably will be reimbursed by the other members of the group when the tickets are bought. But, between the time the arrangements were made and the actual day of the concert something comes up and you decide not to attend the concert. Are you still liable for the cost of the tickets that your non-assertive friend has bought? You contact your friend and explain or excuse yourself from the concert. What is likely to be her response? If she is non-assertive, she will just say something like "Oh, I understand. No, you don't need to pay me for the ticket you're not going to use. Maybe we can get together some other time. Maybe *I* can find someone else to use the ticket." Why should she try to find someone else to go? You're the one who ordered the ticket. She doesn't make much more money in her job than you do. You still owe her for the ticket, but because she is non-assertive, she is very likely to be stuck with the unpaid ticket. The situation produces resentment on her part. She did not have her goals met. The ticket is not paid for. And she is likely to come away from the exchange with you with a lowered self-esteem because she would not speak up and demand that you pay for the ticket. Such is the picture of the non-assertive individual.

Aggressive Behavior. The aggressive individual responds just the opposite way. This is the kind of individual who takes no notice of the goals of others, but is very conscious of her own and who will attempt to gain her goals without any regard to others feelings or responses. This individual I envision as one who wades into a crowd with elbows out, striking anyone who happens to cross her path. She uses whatever methods she can to manipulate her partner to gain her goal. I know you have seen this individual in action: A test is returned in class and the aggressive person did not get the grade she thought she should. Rather than wait to talk with the professor after class, or at a convenient time, she begins a diatribe in the class against what she thinks is unfair treatment of her by the professor. She produces defensiveness on the part of the professor and runs a great risk of being tossed out on her ear, or being dropped from the class as a malcontent. She may even get the professor to admit that the grade was too low (simply to shut her up), but the resentment she fosters will certainly take a long time to heal. The result of her aggressive behavior may be that she feels good by getting things off her chest, but the bad feelings she has created will be evident to all who hear the scene, and will often come back to

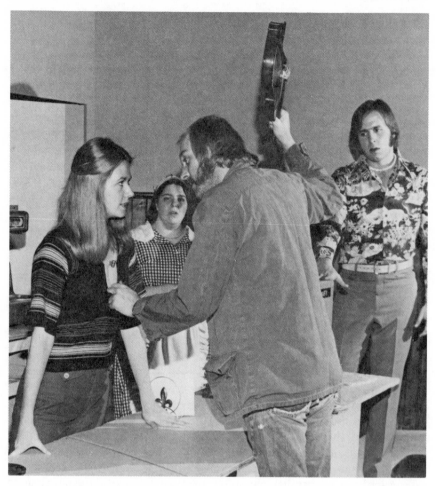

haunt her in her private moments when she thinks of the hostile way she behaved, therefore producing a lowering of her own self-esteem. Aggression may not be the most satisfactory behavior to use for conflict resolution.

Passive Aggressive Behavior. This behavior is odd because it uses both aggressive and non-assertive elements. This kind of action in conflict uses "games" which drives the partner crazy! Dr. George Bach appropriately calls these passive aggressive ploys *crazymakers* . When we fight with someone we know quite well, we know enough information about them to be able to hurt them very effectively. We know how our partners respond to certain situations and the tools of our trade are so carefully used that we are certain that this kind of manipulation will produce the desired effect; i.e., we will win the day. These "crazymakers" include guiltmaking (Don't stay home with me, Go on to your party. I'll be home alone in this big house, but don't think of me!), blamer (It's your fault we ran out of gas!), mind-reader (Wipe that look off your face! I know what you're thinking!), Benedict Arnold (You know what my husband did in bed last night?), the kitchen sinker (You remember what you did last New Year's Eve?) — all of these techniques only rile the partner; they do not attempt to find the solution to the problem at hand. You can probably come up with some you and your partners use which are not on Dr. Bach's list. The point of these "games" is that the actual issue is ignored while you get a good dig into your partner. It is a way of wearing away his self-esteem so that he will be more vulnerable to attack and hence an easier target for your barbs. Notice, however, that the conflict does not get resolved. (For a complete list of *crazymakers,* check Appendix).

Assertive Behavior. This is a type of behavior which takes into account your partner's needs as well as your own. You have goals, but so does your partner in any conflict. For the relationship to remain strong and satisfying both of you must come away from the conflict feeling that you have reached a mutual understanding. This is the most difficult posture to maintain because it requires tact, sensitivity, and non-defensive communication. You and your child are arguing over bedtime. As a adult, you assume that you can and must implement the solution. The child needs to go to bed at 8:30! You have the power to implement the edict you have laid down. The child must simply acquiesce. No problem here (as you, the adult, see it). But suppose for the moment that you request from the child (in good active listening) why he wishes to stay up. He says that the program which comes on at 8:30 is one which was mentioned in class and which his teacher will quiz him on the next day. Would it be possible for him to make his lunch the night before, take his bath, shampoo his hair, get in his pajamas and be all ready to jump into bed when the program is over? The household will run smoothly next morning. The jobs will be done. The solution has been reached. Neither party has come away with a loss, but each has gained, and more importantly, each gained a respect for the other and his point of view.

The major drawback with assertive behavior is that it appears to work fine when the partner is a sensitive, caring individual. What happens if you are faced with the office bully or the corporate fathead who is not interested in anything but his own ego satisfaction? Again, this behavior can work. You merely stick to your guns. Let me restate that. You simply repeat your request with sufficient background information to allow your partner to understand your point of view. You draw the picture of the possibilities of your solution which could work if given a chance. Here we approach the area of negotiation, an art which traders in the Near East and South America are masters at, but which strikes the average citizen of USA as boring, or useless. If you enter a bazaar in Turkey or Beirut and find a carpet you fancy, how do you determine the price you will pay? There is a price quoted to you, but if you understand their culture, you will take that price as only a starting point for the bargaining. The final price you pay for the carpet is a matter of negotiation and the Americans who will take the time and effort to bargain are respected for that quality in these cultures. Why does it seem so difficult for us to apply the same principle to our everyday relationships which occur time after time in which bargaining and negotiation would enhance results?

Assertive behavior does not mean just giving in to the partner. That's non-assertive behavior, and we've already seen the "pay-off" for that posture. The key is not being dragged into a defensive atmosphere in which neither party will gain and both stand to lose. You can fight fairly without the use of crazymakers. You can treat your partner with respect and attempt to understand and appreciate his goals. Here are a few suggestions about resolving conflicts in an equitable, rational way.

Ways to Resolve Conflicts

Set Up the Atmosphere for Resolution. In the chapter on perception you found that hunger, fatigue, and time of day all make a difference about how your partner responds. Bear all these things in mind when you are setting up a time for your partner and you to talk through a problem. Set the date to your mutual advantage. One of my students said one time "I don't want to make a date for a fight!" That is not what you are doing. You are trying to make a date for a *resolution,* quite a different thing. Attempt to keep the atmosphere non-defense producing. There may be something that she does which irritates you, but there are certainly things which you do that irritate her, too. Pick a place where your partner can feel at ease with sufficient quiet for you to hear and understand each other.

Keep to One Problem. This session that you are setting up is not going to be a time when you will settle all the disputes of the years of your relationship. Stick to *one* topic. Oscar, mentioned earlier in this chapter, will not get the chance to correct all *ten* things Felix does which drive him crazy. As peripheral topics come up in conversation (and they will!) table them for a later time. Just work out one problem at a time, and if your efforts are satisfactory, the resolution will provide good ground-work for future problem solutions.

Be Sensitive to your Partner's Needs. Here is where assertiveness rather than aggression pays off. By consistently being aware of what your partner is trying to accomplish, and thoroughly explaining your own goals you stand a chance of meeting part of both yours and your partner's goals. To assume that you will come away from this session with all your own needs met is unrealistic. This is the time for negotiation with both of you recognizing and appreciating each other's need to be individuals acting in cooperation.

Develop Your Own Plan for Resolution. Since all human situations are different, it would be presumptuous of us to suggest a solution formula. There is no such thing that we have seen. Each list that we've read in whatever research we've seen includes the basic ingredients we have included here. The time has come for you to use the information you have gained throughout this text all the way from self-concepts of the people involved to the active listening which you will try to employ. Remember you are the one who must survive. But you do not exist in a vacuum. Your life is inescapably linked with others and they are just as complex and sensitive as you are. No pat answers or magic incantations will allow you to avoid the responsibility you have to make the best of the relationships you have. The ball is in your court. If it takes two to tango and fight, it certainly takes two to find a resolution to the fight. Conflicts give us an opportunity to see just how kind and loving we can be. If this sounds like Pollyanna, so be it, but having lost a few and won a few in my time, I have come to the conclusion that the fights I remember most are the ones which both of us won!

Let's look again at the example of the two farmers from the first chapter. When the horse was found in the bean patch, how could the bean farmer have opened the discussion so as not to produce the defensive response he did from the horse owner? What is the first priority? Get the horse back to the pasture and mend the fence. If the bean farmer had assisted in corralling the horse, the horse owner might be more willing to investigate the damage done by his animal. The damaged beans are not going to disappear. Plenty of time to assess the damage after the horse is removed. The question "What are you going to do about the damage to my beans?" is irrelevant right at that time. Had the bean farmer been sensitive for just a moment to the obvious embarrassment of the horse owner, both men might have gotten satisfaction. The question only served to anger and further embarrass the horse owner. We're not letting the horse owner off the hook, however. His response of "Sue me!" was just as inefficient. Rather than hear the underlying concern on the part of the bean farmer, the horse owner assumed an attack was being made on his ability to keep his animal corralled, his ability to build an adequate fence, even his honesty and fairness as a neighbor who responsibly pays for damage which was caused by his animal. The two men could have reached a resolution by setting up the atmosphere for a resolution. Maybe just as the horse was caught and was being taken back is not the time to bring up the question of retribution. Perhaps a comment like 'Let's get the horse into the barn, and then see what we can do about the fence and the beans,'' would have been a more reasonable and supportive opener. The major problem with the exchange was a basic lack of sensitivity of both farmers to the other's needs and goals.

Conclusion

For the rest of your life you will be facing and solving conflicts. You can approach these conflicts with a dread and fear which incapacitates and leaves you feeling hurt and resentful blaming the world and all around you for treating you in a shabby fashion, or you can approach each potential conflict situation with confidence in yourself and your partner to be able to find a way out of your difficulties. Regard these temporary hassles as part of the natural order of things which provide you with an opportunity to use your skills of survival—interpersonal communication: a free exchange of thoughts, feelings, and ideas. With love, care, and tact you and your partner can respect the other's right to grow and develop as individuals sharing a world made better by interaction, cooperation, and communication.

Bibliography

Alberti, Robert E. and Michael L. Emmons. *Your Perfect Right.* San Luis Obispo, California: Impact, 1970.

Butler, Pamela. *Self-Assertion for Women.* San Francisco: Canfield Press, 1976.

Fensterheim, Herbert and Jean Baer. *Don't Say Yes When You Want to Say No.* New York: Dell Publishing Co., Inc., 1975.

Fisher, Roger and Willaim Ury. Getting to Yes: *Negotiating Agreement Without Giving In.* Boston: Houghton Mifflin, 1981.

Galvin, Kathleen M. and Bernard J. Brommel. *Family Communication: Cohesion and Change.* 2nd Ed. Glenview, IL: Scott, Forsman and Co., 1968.

Gordon, Thomas. *P.E.T.: Parent Effectiveness Training.* New York: Peter H. Wyden, Inc., 1970.

O'Neill Nena and George O'Neill. *Shifting Gears: Finding Security in a Changing World.* New York: M. Evans and Co., Inc., 1974.

Rubin, Theodore Issac. *The Angry Book.* New York: Macmillan, 1969.

Smith, Manual J. *When I Say No, I Feel Guilty.* New York: Bantam Books, 1975.

Appendix A

WEASEL-WORDERS THINK SOFTER SPEECH IS SAFER SPEECH

Don Boxmeyer

> I used to think I was poor. Then they told me I was not poor but needy. Then they told me it was self-defeating to think of myself as needy; I was deprived. Then they told me underprivileged was overused. I was disadvantaged.
> I still don't have a dime, but I have a great vocabulary.
> — *Jules Feiffer, Culture cartoonist (culturoonist?).*

Feiffer's fellow is the victim of a "euphemismist," a professional weasel-worder who knows softer speech is safer speech even though it's dumb. He's like the forest products industry spokesman who says his boys are going out to "maniipulate the vegetation." What ever happened to "cut timber?"

The American language is laced with euphemisms, a word itself that is something like the sound a person makes when he falls off the roof. To use a euphemism is simply a fancy way of avoiding painful reality.

George Orwell, author of "1984," created a classic euphemism for The Man Who Wants To Avoid Trouble At All Costs:

"*A not unblack* dog was chasing a not unsmall rabbit across a not ungreen field."

Professional euphemismists and weasel-worders (Theodore Roosevelt was fond of tossing about the phrase, weasel words, to describe vacuous speech) run the world and they order the way you live.

They sell clothes and trinklets out of "boutiques," instead of stores. They open garages and fix autos over "lubritoriums,"

Reprinted by permission of Globe-Democrat-Knight News Service.

instead of grease pits. They own the phone company and give you "directory assistance" rather than information. They become "funeral directors," instead of morticians or undertakers, and they practice "grief therapy" when they talk about their customers in every term other than the dead.

Why?

"At first glance," wrote linguist Mario Pei, "it is the desire not to shock or offend. That is at the root of euphemisms."

"At this point in time; in this time frame"

"C'mon Bessy, it's time to go to the lounging shed."

Weasel-worders use "purr-r-r and grr-r-r words," one writer said, words that either soothe the listener to sleep or antagonize him. By design. You're supposed to think more kindly of a used car when the advertiser croons that it is "previously owned." When municipal housing officials find a vacant lot in an old neighborhood, they develop the property with "infill housing."

In his "Double-Speak in America," linguist Pei described a new language proposed by an economist to replace labor-management terms the economist considered "grr-r-r" words. Among his suggestions were: "cease to purchase" (for boycott); "work cessation on premises" (for sit-down strike); "directive improvement" (for discipline); and "equitable compensation" (for living wage). The word "labor" itself, the economist suggested, should be replaced by "earning roster," Pei wrote of the economist's new language in 1973. There is, at present, no sign that any of his suggestions have taken hold.

But nowhere do weasel words flourish more than in politics and government. New York Times columnist William Safire produced the "New Language of Politics" and was compelled to expand it to the 809-page "Political Dictionary" largely because the weasel-word business is so good.

Politicians, Safire muses, will do everything to court the vote of the old folks except remind them that they are old. An Esquire magazine cartoon, he recalled, showed an old man shouting at his television set; "Call me gramps, call me an old fogey — call me anything except a senior citizen!"

Former Secretary of Agriculture (and former governor of Minnesota) Orville Freeman used to speak of "concessional exports." He was talking about exports of grain and wheat to countries that didn't pay for them. Orville's use of "concessional exports" was a soft way of saying this country was getting stiffed. Other agricultural experts decided that fancy cow barns (ones with piped-in music) should be described as "milking parlors" or "lounging sheds."

The U.S. Department of Labor in 1977 decided to eliminate age and sex barriers in its list of occupations. It invented such new jobs as "bat handler" for bat boy, "children's tutor" for governess, and "repairer" for repairman. Faced with deciding what to call people who wait on tables, Safire said, the department's weasel-worders came up with the "waiter-waitress."

There's a strange, relatively new language in the intelligence community, compiled in 1976 by a Senate investigative committee, that Safire calls "CIA-ese," or spookspeak. Included in the glossary are such innocuous phrases as "executive action" (which generally means assassination); "Black bag job" (illegal entry and search for documents); "mole" (a friendly agent placed in another country's intelligence system); "fluttering" (to give one's own agents lie detector tests to determine their loyalty); and, of course, "plumbing" (the establishment of an entire clandestine network).

"Plumbing," of course, brings to mind the Watergate era and the lush forests of euphemisms and weasel words that grew in its shadow.

"Watergate came to mean a drama on the grandest scale," Safire writes, "of a search for the 'smoking gun' by the 'straight arrows,' of the 'firestorm' that followed the 'Saturday night massacre' of the good guys, of the 'stonewalling' about 'dirty tricks' and the 'White House horrors' by the 'Big Enchilada, ...' " (The "Big Enchilada," of course, was Attorney General John Mitchell, given the nickname by top Nixon aide John Ehrlichman.)

Another popular White House euphemism was "the whole ball of wax," meaning the entire situation. Shortly after the election of Jimmy Carter as president in 1976, Ronald Reagan demonstrated a charming ability to mangle even simple euphemisms: "They've (the Republicans) got the whole enchilada now," said Reagan.

Watergate also produced such enduring euphemisms as "hanging tough" and the "limited modified hangout route" for not talking. In the end, it was the Nixon entourage that found itself "twisting slowly, slowly in the wind." America was constantly reminded of "the bottom line," what someone had done some "dove tailing," somebody else was "playing hardball," another fellow was "biting the bullet," and it was all happening "at this point in time; in this time frame."

You got the impression these fellows were paid by the word.

One language expert, Penn State professor Gerald Phillips, once coined a nice new euphemism. He offered the word "khulygas" to determine how quickly the use of a new word could spread. He forgot, however, to give the word a meaning. It's still a wonderfully available substitute for anything that you'd like to have go purr-r-r or grr-r-r.

Appendix B

CRAZYMAKERS: INDIRECT AGGRESSION

The avoider   The avoider refuses to fight. When a conflict arises, he'll leave, fall asleep, pretend to be busy at work, or keep from facing the problem in some other way. This behavior makes it very difficult for the partner to express his feelings of anger, hurt, etc., because the avoider won't fight back. Arguing with an avoider is like trying to box with a person who won't even put up his gloves.

The pseudoaccommodator   The pseudoaccommodator refuses to face up to a conflict either by giving in or by pretending that there's nothing at all wrong. This really drives the partner, who definitely feels there's a problem, crazy and causes him to feel both guilt and resentment toward the accommodator.

The guiltmaker   Instead of saying straight out that she doesn't want or approve of something, the guiltmaker tries to change her partner's behavior by making him feel responsible for causing pain. The guiltmaker's favorite line is "It's o.k., don't worry about me. ..." accompanied by a big sigh.

The subject changer   Really a type of avoider, the subject changer escapes facing up to agression by shifting the conversation whenever it

approaches an area of conflict. Because of his tac-
tics, the subject changer and his partner never
have the chance to explore their problem and do
something about it.

The distracter   Rather than come out and express
his feelings about the object of his dissatisfaction,
the distracter attacks other parts of his partner's
life. Thus he never has to share what's really on
his mind and can avoid dealing with painful parts
of his relationships.

The mind reader   Instead of allowing her partner
to express her feelings honestly, the mind reader
goes into character analysis, explaining what the
other person really means or what's wrong with
the other person. By behaving this way the mind
reader refuses to handle her own feelings and
leaves no room for her partner to express himself.

The trapper   The trapper plays an especially dirty
trick by setting up a desired behavior for her partner, and then when it's met, attacking the very
thing she requested. An example of this technique
is for the trapper to say "Let's be totally honest
with each other," and then when the partner shares
his feelings, he finds himself attacked for having
feelings that the trapper doesn't want to accept.

The crisis tickler   This person almost brings
what's bothering him to the surface, but he never
quite comes out and expresses himself. Instead
of admitting his concern about the finances he
innocently asks "Gee, how much did that cost?",
dropping a rather obvious hint but never really
dealing with the crisis.

The gunnysacker   This person doesn't respond
immediately when she's angry. Instead, she puts
her resentment into her gunnysack, which after a
while begins to bulge with large and small gripes.
Then, when the sack is about to burst, the gunny-

sacker pours out all her pent-up aggressions on the overwhelmed and unsuspecting victim.

The trivial tyrannizer Instead of honestly sharing his resentments, the trivial tyrannizer does things he knows will get his partner's goat — leaving dirty dishes in the sink, clipping his fingernails in bed, belching out loud, turning up the television too loud, and so on.

The joker Because she's afraid to face conflicts squarely, the joker kids around when her partner wants to be serious, thus blocking the expression of important feelings.

The beltliner Everyone has a psychological "beltline," and below it are subjects too sensitive to be approached without damaging the relationship. Beltlines may have to do with physical characteristics, intelligence, past behavior, or deeply ingrained personality traits a person is trying to overcome. In an attempt to "get even" or hurt his partner the beltliner will use his intimate knowledge to hit below the belt, where he knows it will hurt.

The blamer The blamer is more interested in finding fault than in solving a conflict. Needless to say, she usually doesn't blame herself. Blaming behavior almost never solves a conflict and is an almost surefire way to make the receiver defensive.

The contract tyrannizer This person will not allow his relationship to change from the way it once was. Whatever the agreements the partners had as to roles and responsibilities at one time, they'll remain unchanged. "It's your job to…feed the baby, wash the dishes, discipline the kids…"

The kitchen sinker This person is so named because in an argument he brings up things that are totally off the subject ("everything but the kitchen sink"): the way his partner behaved last New Year's eve, the unbalanced checkbook, bad breath — anything.

The withholder   Instead of expressing her anger honestly and directly, the withholder punishes her partner by keeping back something — courtesy, affection, good cooking, humor, sex. As you can imagine, this is likely to build up even greater resentments in the relationship.

The Benedict Arnold   This character gets back at his partner by sabotage, by failing to defend him from attackers, and even by encouraging ridicule or disregard from outside the relationship.

GLOSSARY

Abstractions: Words that are not specific enough to describe the true intent of the message.

Active Listening: Thomas Gordon's set of specific skills used when someone comes to you with a problem. (See Chapter Four.)

Advising: Giving solutions to a problem.

Aggressive Behavior: Taking no notice of the goals of others, but attempting to gain goals without regard to other's feelings or responses.

Ambiguity: Choosing the wrong word deliberately clouding the message.

Ambushing: Listening to get information to use against the speaker.

Analyzing: Interpreting messages sent.

Apathy: A defense mechanism that shows lack of concern or the opposite of what we truly feel.

Artifacts: The clothing, hair style, jewelry and accessories we wear.

Assertive Behavior: Behavior that takes into account your partner's needs as well as your own.

Certainty: Defensive behavior caused by acting as if you are *always right*.

Channel: The media (air, phone, TV) through which a message is sent.

Compensate: A defense mechanism that ignores the subject at hand and turns discussion to the speaker's strong point.

Conflict: A blanket term covering any disagreement from trivial matters to war.

Connotations: The cluster of feelings and images which surrounds a word.

Control: Defense-producing behavior in which we play 'boss'' and tell others what to do.

Crazymakers: Ploys and devices used in conflict which raise defensiveness and cloud the issues of the conflict. Ways of fighting "dirty" that drive our partners crazy.

Decode: The process of turning a symbol back into a mental image.

Defensive Listening: Taking innocent remarks as personal attacks.

Defensiveness: Actions taken to protect the public image.

Denotative Meanings: The dictionary definition of a word: what the word generally means.

Description: A supportive behavior that cuts down on defensiveness by using "I" language to express how something affects us.

Displacement: A defense mechanism that takes out anger on someone not involved in the cause of the defensive situation.

Efficient Messages: Communication that includes enough information for our partners to really understand us. (See Chapter 1).

Emotionally-Loaded Words: Words that raise strong feelings when heard: "Commie," "Fag", "America."

Empathy: Supportive behavior that reduces defensiveness by listening to another's verbals and nonverbals.

Encode: The process of turning a mental image into a symbol believed to be understandable by another person.

Entertainment Syndrome: The belief that you do not have to listen to anything that is not amusing or interesting.

Environment: An individual's point of view made up of his/her background, language, culture, and experience.

Equality: Supportive behavior which decreases defensiveness by treating others as human beings.

Euphemisms: Words which "soften" the event or function being described.

Evaluate: Defense-producing behavior in which we pass judgment using "you" language.

Fantasy: A defense mechanism which retreats into daydreaming.

Feedback: Message verification sent from person to person.

Flower of Evil: The development of resentment which grows petal by petal, gripe by gripe.

Hearing: The process of perceiving sound: reverberation of sound waves in the ear.

"I" Language: Supportive phrases that lessen defensiveness such as "I think you could do better" or "I feel upset when you don't call."

Insensitive Listening: Taking what is said literally without applying the nonverbal implications to the message.

Insulated Listening: Tuning out when a subject is not to our liking.

Interpersonal Communication: The exchange of thoughts and feelings between two or more people.

Johari Window: Luft's and Ingham's model used for examining self-disclosure.

Judging: Evaluation of what is said.

Kinesics: Body language which includes facial expressions, gestures and posture.

Listening: The ability to pay attention: the willingness to understand oral communication.

Pseudolistening: Pretending to listen.

Maslow's Hierarchy of Needs: Psychologist Abraham Maslow's five categories of human desires which include physical, security, social, self-esteem, and self-actualization.

Neutrality: Defense-producing behavior in which we ignore others.

Noise: Any interference with listening or hearing what is said: physical, external, and internal.

Non-Assertive Behavior: Allowing any and everybody to walk all over you without putting up any kind of defense.

Nonverbal Communication: Actions, facial expressions, body movement, appearance, tone of voice that add meaning to verbal messages.

Paralinguals: Sounds we make apart from language: volume, pitch, speed.

Perception: The act of categorizing and interpreting sense data.

Passive Agressive Behavior: A defensive posture which subtly undermines your partner's self-esteem. (See Crazymakers.)

Private Self: What we believe to be true about ourselves kept to ourselves.

Problem Orientation: Supportive behavior that involves the cooperation of all involved to find a mutually satisfactory solution to a problem.

Projection: A defense mechanism that blames someone else.

Provisionalism: Supportive behavior that lessens defensiveness by considering other's ideas.

Proxemics: The distance kept between people: intimate, social, and business.

Public Self: How we wish others to see us.

Questioning: Responding with leading questions.

Rationalization: A defense mechanism that gives a logical, but untrue explanation for our behavior.

Receiver: The person attempting to understand the communication sent.

Recognition: Becoming aware of present habits.

Refusal: Dedication to stopping poor listening habits.

Replacement: Substituting positive listening habits for old ineffectual ones.

Repression: A defense mechanism that disavows any connection with the situation.

Selective Listening: Tuning in only to subjects we are interested in.

Self-Disclosure: The act of deliberately revealing your thoughts and feelings as they occur.

Self-Fulfilling Prophecy: A strongly held belief which dictates the outcome of an event.

Self-Concept: The beliefs a person holds to be true about him or herself.

Semantics: The study of word usage.

Sender: The person initiating communication.

Spontaneity: Supportive behavior that employs honesty in making requests.

Stagehogging: Not listening due to constant talking.

Strategy: Defensive behavior that manipulates others by determining before the conversation the response of the partner.

Superiority: Defense-producing behavior characterized by behaving as if you were better than others.

Supporting: Assuring the partner that "all will be for the best."

Verbal Aggression: The defense mechanism that involves raising the voice, accusing, and name calling.

Undoing: The defense mechanism which attempts to "make-up" for a perceived wrong-doing: sending flowers, taking to dinner, etc.

"You" Language: Accusitory, defense-producing phrases like "You should have done better!" or "You are lazy."